Thinkers

Revised Second Edition

Michael Clay Thompson

Royal Fireworks Press
Unionville, New York

This book is dedicated
to the memory of Kenneth Clark,
whose teaching continues
in his books and *Civilisation* series.

Royal Fireworks Press
First Ave, PO Box 399
Unionville, NY 10988
845 726 4444
email: mail@rfwp.com
website: rfwp.com

ISBN: 978-0-88092-218-0

Printed and bound in the United States of America using vegetable-based
inks and environmentally-friendly cover coatings on recycled, acid-free
paper by Royal Fireworks Press

Table of Contents

INTRODUCTION

This book is called *Thinkers* as a triple reference. Education is all about thinkers. The thinkers described in these chapters, such as George Eliot, Kenneth Clark, Jonathan Swift, Frederick Douglass, and Kaye Gibbons, not only form part of the essential contact that makes an educated mind, but they also serve as edifying prototypes of the thinking mind. To read them is to ride the stream of exploratory thought, whether it descends the rocky channels of fiction or the clear-winding rills of nonfiction.

The ultimate audience for this book is a second group of thinkers: students who are learning about the life of the mind and who think they want to think. Intellectually motivated students are among the finest thinkers in the world. They have open minds and a readiness for surprise, and the shorelines of their minds are unspoiled by prior biases.

The third group of thinkers is the teachers (who may be parents) who will read this book as a way to energize their own thinking about the ideas discussed and who either may use these essays to prepare for class or to provide them directly to their students.

In these essays I hope that the reader will see thoughtful books and films as a kind of extential algebra, each book providing another equation for describing our world and our life in it.

Note for the 2012 Revised Edition: This book was originally written in the mid-1990s, and a number of references are now noticeably out of date. I have decided not to update any of these because I would only have to update them every several years endlessly and because it is interesting to remember where things stood just before the turn of the millennium. The years have given the book extra value as a snapshot.

ONE

A History of Knowledge

Charles Van Doren

Are you ready for a quiz? What do you mean, you did not know you would have to take a quiz? Yes, you have to take it. Who do the following descriptions describe?

1. Erasmus called him *homnium horarum homo*, a man for all seasons. In 1516 he published *Utopia*, a word that he coined for the purpose, and in this book he imagined a better world where people were equal and everyone believed in a good God. In time Henry VIII had him executed.

2. He said the secret was *saper vedere*, to know how to see. And see he did. He left thousands of notes and sketches on every imaginable subject, as well as a handful of paintings that are among the great treasures of the world.

3. He created a school in Athens, teaching his students in the *Stoa Poikile*, or painted colonnade, and hence the name of his philosophy, *stoicism*, which taught that human happiness comes from conforming to the will of divine reason. We are happy if we accept what is and do not long for what is not.

4. When he and his Persian army arrived at the Hellespont, the waves were high, forcing the army to delay its crossing. Enraged, he commanded his soldiers to whip the waves for their insubordination.

In his humane and accessible *A History of Knowledge*, Charles Van Doren discusses these and several hundred other individuals who have contributed to the making of the modern mind. Van Doren's survey of ideas begins with the ancient world and continues through Planck's constant and Heisenberg's uncertainty principle. He discusses not only Occidental thought but Oriental thought as well.

Oh, you want to know the answers to the quiz? All right, the author of *Utopia* was Thomas More. Leonardo da Vinci said the secret was *saper vedere*. Zeno was the Stoic, and that fool Xerxes whipped the waves.

As the title suggests, Van Doren's discussion focuses not on the trodden paths of world political and military history that students have wearily tramped in every textbook—as though all people do is govern and fight—but on the part of human history that is so often missing from students' history texts: ideas. Ideas are the ozone hole in our curricular atmosphere. Our neoRoman pragmatism—sculpture is for wimps, real men build arches!—leads us into a shallow, reportorial approach to history; we limit our texts to history's plot, the who-what-where-when, and we ignore the why. Well, any competent English teacher will tell you that a discussion limited to plot gets not at the thought. Our understanding of the world must be conceptual, not bicep-tual.

What? Oh, all right, here are some more thinkers to test your knowledge of intellectual history:

5. She not only wrote the first fully adult work of fiction, but lived independently in opposition to the mores of her age. Respectable people drove her from respectable England because she was not married to her companion, but she counterattacked with books that exposed the small-mindedness of Victorian life.

6. Everything, he decided, is composed of a number of small particles—or atoms, as he called them—whose

connections and dissolutions explain the arising and passing of all phenomena.

7. He had composed hundreds of the world's most superb musical works by the age of twenty-five, and died ten years later in abject poverty, to be buried in a pauper's grave.

8. His greatest contribution was the set of three laws of planetary motion that solved the problem of epicycles and eccentric orbits once and for all. These three laws are still valid and bear his name.

Give up? The anti-Victorian novelist was George Eliot. Democritus developed the atomic theory (though Thales realized before him that there must be some uniform substratum for material existence). Mozart died in poverty, and Kepler figured out how planets move.

Beethoven once said that for the person "who understands my music, all the problems of life will be solved." And after listening to the *Pastoral* symphony, we might almost agree (no, not the *Eroica* symphony—too strident), but even though *A History of Knowledge* is a symphony of ideas, it will not solve all the problems of life—even intellectual life. The ice-mind David Hume, for example, who has been called the greatest philosopher to have written in the English language, is not even mentioned. Nor is Wittgenstein. Nor Voltaire.

And so *A History of Knowledge* is something less than a pocket university. It is, however, a dazzling performance by Van Doren. If Wittgenstein is not there, then Avicenna is. And Seneca. And Tacitus. Averroës is there, and Montaigne, and Erasmus. If Van Doren passes over Hume, he lingers over Newton, offering one of the best concise statements of Newton's contribution to the mind of the world. And Van Doren has depth; he is not star-struck in the presence of alpha-geniuses like Newton:

> Newton, with all his brilliance, did not understand why the force of gravity acts as it does; that is, he did not know what gravity is. Nor do we. He only knew that it acted the way it did. He was right about that, to his eternal credit. But the reasons of things, as Pascal might have called them, still lie hid in night.

One of the best features of *A History of Knowledge* is that Van Doren forcefully pushes his discussion into the 20th century, providing students (and their teachers) with a strong discussion of modern thought. Van Doren discusses DNA, modern findings about the universe, Heisenberg's Uncertainty Principle, computers, the challenge of AIDS, and genetic engineering. But he also discusses the arts: Picasso, Braque, Pollock, and Rothko are there. There is a discussion of Forster, and even of Samuel Beckett.

What, you want four more thinkers? Well, as Old Kinderhook, Martin Van Buren, wrote, *OK*.

9. He mockingly described the Idols of the Tribe, those intellectual faults that are common to all human beings, such as the tendency to oversimplify, which makes us see more order than is there, or the tendency to prefer novelty, which sometimes makes us discard good theory for new theory.

10. With his friend Petrarch, he deliberately set about to create a Renaissance of ancient literature and knowledge, and the two of them successfully devoted the remainder of their lives to the project.

11. His great message consisted of Four Noble Truths. This first is that human existence is full of suffering. The

second is that our difficulty and pain are caused by selfish desire. The third is that we can free ourselves from pain, and the fourth is the way.

12. He inspired a fervor that would lead his followers to conquer the Byzantine and Persian empires and create a land empire rivaling both in size and organization the Roman empire at its greatest.

Yes, the Idol-mocker was Frances Bacon. Petrarch's Renaissance buddy was Bocaccio. Buddha enunciated the Four Noble Truths, and Muhammad's followers swept up two great empires.

Students who have read Van Doren's book have angrily asked why their history textbooks never told them these things. What is the answer? (We fear that the real answer would test our tolerance for the bleak.) For anyone who believes in real education, *A History of Knowledge* is a solid contribution.

TWO

Civilisation

Kenneth Clark

How often have you dreamed of a time machine, one that would let you go back and see the dinosaurs, or witness thundering Waterloo from a protected hilltop, or walk up the mount to hear the Sermon? With a time machine, we could go to see Plato, or Socrates, or Amelia Earhart, or Joan of Arc. We could hide and watch Henry the VIII or travel across unpaved Europe to meet Catherine the Great. We could go to Assissi and see Francis. We could talk to Harriet Tubman and hear the stories. We could look at the gentle face of Lincoln or at the awesomely handsome face of Frederick Douglass. We could meet Leonardo and watch him paint Mona.

Just imagine.

But there is no time machine.

Is there?

Well, what if we had beautiful video documentaries of these individuals, and we could see their real faces, and hear their real voices, and watch the movements of their hands as they taught us, through the medium of video, what they wanted us to know?

By some unlikely and fortuitous miracle, that is what we have in the case of Kenneth Clark and his improbable masterpiece, *Civilisation*, which is available today both in book and (better) video form.

Kenneth Clark—Lord Clark of Saltwood, that is—was nothing less than the Director of the National

Gallery in London, and the Surveyor of the King's Pictures. Educated at Winchester and Trinity College, Oxford, Lord Clark had perhaps the most distinguished and admired career of any modern art historian. He was Slade Professor of Fine Arts at Oxford from 1946 until 1950, and he was the Chairman of the Arts Council of Great Britain, as well as a Trustee of the British Museum. And much more.

He may actually have been the most cultivated man of our century.

To have Kenneth Clark as your art teacher would be like, oh, having A.C. Bradley as your Shakespeare instructor.

But, see, you can have.

Clark, that is, as your teacher.

Through video.

Old video, too.

Even though *Civilisation* has been reissued in a restored, affordable format, no one would mistake *Civilisation* for a glossy recent product or Kenneth Clark for a contemporary man. Heavens, no. He is hopelessly wrong for our time and was probably an anachronism even in 1969 when *Civilisation* debuted. With his Tweedle Dum body, and his funny crooked teeth, and his partial head of hair, and his cute silk handkerchief stuck aristocratically in his elegant pocket, and his heartbreaking sincere smile, and his gentle voice, he is an anti-hero, as removed as possible from the Age of Schwarzenegger. In almost Chaplinesque fashion, he pops up happy in front of the landmarks of western culture: here he is in front of the Pont du Gard aqueduct near Nîmes, stepping over stones; here he is peeping out tiny from the pedestal of Michelangelo's colossal *David*, pleased with himself for having thought of it. Here he is, admiring a Viking ship, which he calls the symbol of Atlantic Man (the Greek temples were his symbols of Mediterranean Man).

And everywhere, he casts a light of admiration on the objects of attention, the paintings, the sculpture, the illuminated manuscripts, the monastery arcades, the cathedrals.

If this were only a personal tour of the fine art of the Western world, it would be a privilege to come along with Kenneth Clark as our guide. But *Civilisation* is more than a televised art lecture; it is a controlled and penetrating examination of, well, civilization.

With the mushroom cloud rising lurid in the background, Clark considers that it is a good time to understand what it means to be civilized. We can no longer afford, he thinks, the alternative.

And of the options available to humanity for understanding civilization, Clark argues, the best is art, for art reveals truth. Clark quotes Ruskin on the trustworthiness of art and adds, "If I had to say which was telling the truth about society, a speech by a Minister of Housing or the actual buildings put up in his time, I should believe the buildings."

There it is.

Believe the buildings.

From this lucid beginning, Clark proceeds to examine those human qualities that give civilized life its value, and he does this with a language and style that is as elegant, and refined, as any we are likely to hear. More so.

What does the fall of the mighty Roman empire show us about civilization?

It shows that however complex and solid it seems, it is actually quite fragile. It can be destroyed. What are its enemies? Well, first of all, fear—fear of war, fear of invasion, fear of plague and famine, that make it simply not worthwhile constructing things, or planting trees or even planning next year's crops. And fear of the supernatural, which means that you daren't question anything or change anything.

You daren't question.

Well, it is the Interrogative Heroes who become the stars of Clark's survey of western cultural history. He admires the "brilliant, enigmatic" Peter Abelard, who contradicted Anselm's doctrine of unquestioning belief: "By doubting we come to questioning," Abelard reasoned, "And by questioning we perceive the truth." Strange words, Clark subtly observes, to have been written in 1122.

Clark leads us through the ruins of Greek temples and the Roman roads, through the court of Charlemagne, whose scribes rescued pagan literature from the ravages of time, to the frosty and remote island of Skellig Michael, where Christians hid their cherished faith from the roving barbarian horror. He pauses at Chartres Cathedral, shows us the solidity in Giotto's frescoes, and eulogizes Dante, "a man who is unequaled—the greatest philosophic poet that has ever lived."

Clark takes us to the lovely palace at Urbino, shows us the duke's quarters, and wanders off to Florence, where this business of questions comes up again; Clark quotes the Renaissance art historian Vasari on the spirit of criticism in Florence that makes minds free and discontented with mediocrity, adding:

And this harsh, outspoken competition between Florentine craftsmen not only screwed up technical standards, but also meant that there was no gap of incomprehension between the intelligent patron and the artist. Our contemporary attitude of pretending to understand works of art in order not to appear Philistines would have seemed absurd to the Florentines. They were a tough lot.

Clark admires a tough lot and views the Florentine spirit of criticism as essential in keeping the vigor of civilization alive.

Gradually, Clark takes us past the high water marks of civilization: Michelangelo's chapel ceiling, and Leonardo's notebooks, and Mozart's music. We rediscover Gutenberg, and Erasmus, and Albrecht Dürer, Aldus Manutius, and Raphael, and Descartes, Bacon and Spinoza, and Vermeer. It is an interdisciplinary journey.

But it is Clark's ideas that keep delighting us. He shows us, for example, that civilization depends upon a balance between the "male and female principle." Or, in discussing Baroque Rome, Clark warns against the excesses of grandeur:

The sense of grandeur is no doubt a human instinct, but carried too far, it becomes inhuman. I wonder if a single thought that has helped forward the human spirit has ever been conceived or written down in an enormous room: except, perhaps, in the reading room of the British Museum.

This right-you-are plain sense of Clark's disarms us; we keep expecting lofty pronouncements from the great man who stands beside, or on top of, or underneath these "important" buildings or art works, but Clark is, finally, a deeply human being who uses art in a deeply human way. It is people, Clark sees, who are important.

With art, Clark believes, we can understand ourselves and use what is best in our intelligence to build and continually rebuild not just a culture, but a civilization, and the work of building civilization falls finally not to any system or abstraction, but to the individual human beings who must find in their own humanity the answers to their questions. It is in this light that Clark views the contributions of the great artists, architects, poets, and composers. "Above all," Clark tells us, "I believe in the God-given genius of certain individuals, and I value a society that makes their existence possible."

Civilisation has been called the "documentary by which all others are measured," and now that the film is available in an affordable edition, we can show students why. Not only did *Civilisation* create a new genre of powerful, extensive, profoundly educational documentary, a genre that would be brilliantly used by Jacob Bronowski in *The Ascent of Man* and James Burke in *The Day the Universe Changed*, but *Civilisation* established a precedent of quality that has challenged subsequent thinkers and has provided the new generation of *Homo videoensis* with something worth watching.

And not the least of the benefits of *Civilisation* is the example of Clark himself, a gentle and affable man, courteous and soft-spoken, who provides a salutary contrast to the strong-jawed, ham-fisted action heroes of the cartoons and cartoonish adult adventure films that saturate our popular culture. In Clark's own words, he is a "stick-in-the-mud" who believes in courtesy, "the ritual by which we avoid hurting other people's feelings by satisfying our own egos." In our age of ego-apotheosis, we watch Clark's beautiful film with a feeling of increasing affection, both for him and for his human ideas, values, and questions.

THREE

The Hot Zone

Richard Preston

As the tropical wildernesses of the world are destroyed, previously unknown viruses that have lived undetected in the rain forest for eons are entering human populations. The appearance of AIDS is part of the pattern, and the implications for the future of the human species are terrifying.

Richard Preston's book *The Hot Zone* is not only a sensational best seller that has spawned a mediocre adventure movie, *Outbreak*; it is also a book that combines high drama, cutting-edge science, geography, ethical dilemmas, biology, an understanding about the global interrelationship of various ecological and social systems, information about governmental biohazard defense systems, questions about the future of the human race, and even literary merit.

The Hot Zone, amazingly, is the nonfiction account, first published in the *New Yorker*, of an outbreak of Level 4 biohazard filovirus in Reston, Virginia, within sight of Washington D.C.

Level 4 biohazards are extremely lethal viruses for which there is no cure and which only can be studied at frightful risk in ultrasecure, submarine-like government labs at the CDC, the Center for Disease Control in Atlanta, and at USAMRIID, the United States Army Medical Research Institute of Infectious Diseases at Fort

Detrick in Frederick, Maryland. Scientists who work on Level 4 biohazards must work in space suits, tape the zippers and seams of their clothing, and access the negative-air-pressure lab through a series of locks and decontamination showers designed to kill any virus—hot agent—that moves.

Or, perhaps, does not move.

For that's the point, you see. Virus does not exactly move. It is only semi-alive; it can be frozen, crystallized, boiled or otherwise insulted—unharmed—and can wait dormant in, say, the dust of a cave for tens of thousands of years until a host or a victim makes contact with it. And then, like some evil transforming alien a billion times smaller than we are, the virus resurrects, attacks the cells of the nearest life form, and replicates through horrifying extreme amplification, converting its dying prey into countless billions of itself.

If viruses were three feet long, they would be the most dreaded sort-of-organism on the planet.

But then, they already are.

Preston makes sure that we understand this point—the lethal horror of biosafety Level 4 hot agents. In the first chapter, he describes the symptoms and death of a French immigrant in Zaire who developed a case of Marburg virus, the gentle sibling of the even more lethal Ebola Zaire.

The Frenchman—Preston calls him "Charles Monet"—developed his first symptoms seven days after visiting Zaire's Kitum Cave. The first flu-like symptoms of headache and backache were followed three days later by the rapid collapse of Monet's body as the virus swiftly destroyed his immune system and internal organs. His eyes filled with blood; he developed lesions all over his skin that rapidly turned into spontaneous festering black and yellow bruises; the virus dissolved his connecting tissues, detaching his skin from the organs underneath and leaving his face hanging limp on his head; his internal organs dissolved and died while he was still alive; and he finally crashed and bled, losing blood from all body orifices at once. Not only was there nothing that hospital doctors could do to save him, they had no idea what had happened to him.

Marburg did to Monet in ten days, Preston says, what it takes AIDS ten years to do.

And to get to the hospital, Monet had taken an airplane, in which he was confined in a small space with other passengers.

Fortunately for them, and for the world, Monet only had Marburg. If he had contracted Ebola Zaire, Marburg's ugly stepsibling, things would have gotten serious. Ebola is a "slate-wiper" that kills over ninety percent of its victims, hospitalized or not. Add to this, air travel. Preston writes:

A hot virus from the rain forest lives within a twenty-four-hour plane flight from every city on earth. All of the earth's cities are connected by a web of airline routes. The web is a network. Once a virus hits the net, it can shoot anywhere in a day—Paris, Tokyo, New York, Los Angeles, wherever planes fly. Charles Monet and the life form inside him had entered the net.

If these ideas have captured your attention, consider that they come from chapter one of *The Hot Zone*; in subsequent chapters, Preston describes how in 1989 a hot strain of Ebola filovirus entered the United States in a laboratory monkey and began infecting other monkeys through the air, creating a serious biohazard emergency in Reston, Virginia. Knowing that Ebola Zaire is blindly lethal to all primates, including humans, special teams of medical and armed forces personnel directed by CDC and USAMRIID biohazard experts sealed off the animal laboratory, exterminated all animals in the facility, and chemically "nuked" the facility, leaving it for the moment the most biologically sterile place on earth. Not even a bacterium survived. Or so it was hoped.

This story, for all its gripping drama, is true.

It takes readers to Africa, to Washington, to Virginia. It gives them insight into the frightening work of leading biohazard scientists. It provides information, including electron microscope photographs, about filoviruses. It offers insights into the meaning of the practice of medicine. It explores questions of health and safety from a global perspective. It makes connections between caves, biological organisms, transportation systems, and technology. It shows how a single human artifact, the Kinshasa Highway, can pose a credible threat to the future of humanity. It raises enormous ethical questions about the limits of permissible defense against Level 4 biohazards: At what point do such questions as cruelty to animals and citizens' constitutional rights collide with humanity's right to save itself from biological catastrophe?

And—and this is important—it does all of these things in a context of reading.

In *The Hot Zone*, not only will students have the experience of reading a superb book, but they will be introduced indirectly to the *New Yorker*, no mean advantage. From Preston's book, students can gain an understanding of the *New Yorker*'s sublime standards of accuracy and clarity and be led to other outstanding reading experiences. It is easy to imagine that Preston's riveting *The Hot Zone* could be a thinking student's catalyst for a lifelong interest in the reading stratum offered by the very best periodicals that are routinely read by well-educated people.

One of the most arresting facts of *The Hot Zone* is that the real host of the filoviruses remains unknown. How do monkeys become infected? Does the virus lurk in an insect, in a spider, in a bat? Does it lay dormant in the biological detritus of a cave? Does it exist undiscovered in a strain that would make Ebola Zaire seem benign? Has Ebola virus already escaped Zaire again? Has it permanently taken up residence in multiple global locations?

We do not know.

We only know that we cannot wait passively to see what happens; we must begin taking intelligent precautionary measures in advance. And it would not hurt for our biohazard specialists to be highly gifted scientists, for as Preston's last words remind us, Ebola "will be back."

Talk about future problem solving.

FOUR

A Brief History of Time

Stephen Hawking

A Brief History of Time, by Stephen Hawking. Bantam, New York, 1988. 182 pages.
A Brief History of Time, Video. Paramount, 1992. 84 minutes.
The Making of A Brief History of Time, Video. Paramount, 1993. 30 minutes.

In a Woody Allen movie, a small child is taken to the psychiatrist. Skinny and bespectacled, the child is depressed and inconsolable. "What's wrong?" his mother asks. " I can't do anything with him. Tell the doctor what's wrong." At last, the child responds, and with plaintive wail, he discloses the despair in his mind. "The universe," he cries, "is expanding!"

And we laugh.

The cute incongruity of the child's personal concern over problems so remote to our ordinary thought delights us. In our wisdom, we do not care that the universe is expanding.

But . . .

But the child is right. It is the child who sees the truth. The universe is expanding because it is an explosion, the biggest bang, and we ride the whirling debris in complacent oblivion, not realizing that the explosion may reach the end of its force, when gravity will begin to pull everything back together into the Big Crunch, annihilating every human dream. Yes, this would take place millions of years beyond our own lifetimes, but the death sentence for distant hopes is no less real. And the child, in his gifted vision, knows.

On the cover of *A Brief History of Time*, his bestselling discussion of theoretical physics—yes, bestselling—science superstar Stephen W. Hawking sits paralyzed and bemused in his wheelchair, frail and thin, with the image of the cosmos glittering behind him. Today, Hawking has no voice, cannot write, and has no control over his fragile limbs, and yet he is perhaps the most powerful theoretical physicist in the world. In fact, Hawking holds Newton's chair as Lucasian Professor of Mathematics at Cambridge. Communicating through a computer system that allows him to speak through a synthesized voice by selecting words through a maze of on-screen menus, Hawking continues to work and teach and to generate some of the most extraordinary ideas and questions of our time. And his work is now available both through his "popular book about space and time" and its companion films.

The book presents accessible discussions, using words and illustrations rather than equations, of space, time, the expanding universe, the uncertainty principle, elementary particles, forces of nature, black holes, the origin and fate of the universe, and the unification of physics. There are also sketches of Einstein, Galileo, and Newton. Hawking says that previous literature on these subjects did not really address "the questions that had led me to do research in cosmology and quantum theory: Where did the universe come from? How and why did it begin? Will it come to an end, and if so, how?" With such questions, Hawking reminds us that asking is thinking, in its most active form.

The film version of the book contains much of the most critical language of the book, delivered through Hawking's synthetic voice: WYYY DOOO WEE REEMEMBURR THEE PAZD BUHT NOHT THEE FYOOCHURR? But unlike the book, the film is interspersed with biographical content: photographs of the young Stephen Hawking, his mother's memories, anecdotes from friends and colleagues, and Hawking's own comments about his unique situation. By moving back and forth from Hawking's personal life to his theoretical life, and by the use of beautifully restrained camera work supported by music composed by Philip Glass—Errol Morris improbably creates a film worthy of the book, a book that was believed to be unfilmable. For this reason, the film itself emerges as an independently interesting creative product, and this leads to *The Making of A Brief History of Time*, a documentary that reviews the decisions and techniques involved in translating Hawking's abstractions into film.

As a set of three documents, the book, the film, and the film of the film pack a curricular combination punch that is rarely, or perhaps even never before, available.

The scientific ideas alone are of immense importance. Here are the state-of-the-art theories of ultimate reality, of the nature of being itself, of the mystery called time, of the beginning of what is sometimes called creation. Hawking takes us to the edge, to conclusions where thinking simply fails: "At the big bang itself, the universe is thought to have had zero size, and so to have been infinitely hot." Easy for him to say.

Beyond the scientific ideas, there are other aspects of the book and films that make them essential. Perhaps the most important of these is simply the opportunity to meet Stephen Hawking—not because the story of his handicap adds impressive meaning to his achievement, though it does, but because even if he were physically normal, he is Stephen Hawking. Through film and video technology, we can know one of the great scientists of the world, see him, see his environment, meet his friends and family. Only occasionally does a great scientist write for the layman; we think of Einstein's explanations of relativity and Watson's *The Double Helix*, works that enabled the world to have a glimpse of the experience and vision of great science. Hawking's book and accompanying films take this opportunity even further.

And then of course there is the important story of Hawking's fierce struggle with the enormous handicaps of ALS, known as Lou Gehrig's disease. We cannot watch these films without having new realizations about what such physical conditions do and do not mean. It was, for example, after the onslaught of Hawking's disease that he married, had children, and made his contributions to theoretical physics.

We also find illuminating insights into the nature of genius. In one striking interview, a colleague and former Cambridge classmate relates how he and others worked for weeks on a dozen advanced mathematical problems but were only able to crack two after the most arduous efforts; Hawking, meanwhile, waited until the last day and then worked on the problems alone for an hour, and not knowing the struggle put forth by his classmates, apologized that he had only been able to complete ten. This, the colleague confides, is when he realized that Stephen's order of intelligence set him apart.

Among the greatest benefits of the book and films is the model of free thinking that is illustrated. Here is a first-rank scientist of unchallengeable credibility, asking questions that would be ridiculed by the yahoos of the world. "Why do we remember the past but not the future?" Hawking asks. His very asking is a message of the highest importance, an assertion of our right to challenge foundations and to break the false shackles of the obvious.

Finally, *The Making of a Brief History of Time* offers beautiful secondary considerations, connecting aesthetics, interdisciplinary thinking, problem solving, issues of presentation, and human sensitivities to the facts of the book and first film.

Whatever time is, spend some reading this extraordinary book and viewing the two companion films. You will not remember them until they are in your past.

FIVE

Middlemarch

George Eliot

Among the pantheon of supreme books of the world are a neglected handful that are too rarely read. These books include long masterpieces, such as Cervantes's *Don Quixote*, Tolstoy's *War and Peace*, and Hugo's *Les Miserables*. In English literature, the greatest book to gather unmerited dust is almost certainly *Middlemarch*, the 1871 masterwork of the intellectual giant Mary Anne Evans, known to the world by her *nom de plume*, George Eliot.

George Eliot has been hailed as "the great English novelist of ideas" whose work is a "genuine source of wisdom." Her magnum opus *Middlemarch* appears on few course syllabi, but it has been described as the Victorian era's most impressive novel, as unconventional, as the first fully adult work of fiction, and as a highly intellectual form of art. Charles Van Doren describes *Middlemarch* as pitiless, a novel "that tore away the curtain of Victorian life and revealed its bitter small-mindedness for anyone to see." Not, Van Doren adds, that anyone did see.

As artists do, George Eliot found fiction in fact, and the result was truth. She and her companion George H. Lewes were ostracized by England's good set, who wanted nothing to do with this "strong-minded" woman who lived openly with a married man; never mind that the married man was unable to get a divorce from his lawful wife, who would have two children by another man, and that George and George would live together devotedly until Lewes's death in 1878.

To the heinous charge of being strong-minded—a term of admiration when applied to a man—Mary Anne Evans would have had to plead guilty. All of her life, she had known her own mind and had been willing to change her life in accordance with her convictions, with or without the approval of others. She was an ardent Christian early in her life, but when her observations on the lives of Dissenters and the facts of science led her to doubt the literal truth of the Bible, she strong-mindedly informed her irate father that she would no longer go to church.

Reading widely in English, Spanish, French, Italian, Latin, and German, Eliot strong-mindedly helped to translate D.F. Strauss's *Das Leben Jesu Kritisch Bearbeitet* (*The Life of Jesus Critically Examined*) into English. Her intellectual force was recognized by others, and she was asked to serve as editor of the once prestigious *Westminster Review*, restoring that publication to the glory it had known under its former deity, John Stuart Mill.

Eventually, she met the unhappy journalist, George Henry Lewes, who found in her strong-mindedness a strong mind and who encouraged her to write and to adopt a *nom de homme*—George, say—in order to mollify the rejection of a public that could not comprehend intellectual power in a woman.

Eliot's unconventionality continued to characterize her life until the end. When Lewes died in 1878, the sixty-one-year-old writer gravitated to John Cross, a banker twenty-one years younger than she. They were married on May 6, 1880, and spent their honeymoon in Italy, but after their return to England, Eliot died on December 22 of the same year. Originally buried in Highgate cemetery, she was moved to the happier ground of Westminster Abbey in 1980, one hundred years after her death; a modern public had finally accepted this strong-minded woman.

For anyone whose impressions of Eliot were formed by an adolescent reading of *Silas Marner*, *Middlemarch* may come as a shock. *Silas Marner* might lead one to expect from this writer a sort of fable, somewhat sentimental, illustrating truisms about love being more important than gold.

But *Middlemarch* is no tedious allegory. One encounters it with a certain incredulity and a feeling of vulnerable exposure, as in an alien abduction when one is slapped helplessly onto a strange metal table and probed with frightening instruments of unknown purpose. *Middlemarch* looks right through you; Eliot's vision is penetrating to the point of discomfort. She describes the failing marriage between Rosamond and Lydgate: "Between him and her indeed there was that total missing of each other's mental track, which is too evidently possible even between persons who are continually thinking of each other."

Boom. It is a gaze as Yeats described, blank and pitiless as the sun. Rosamond's indifference to her husband grows until his feeling of abandonment becomes overwhelming: "It seemed that she had no more identified herself with him than if they had been creatures of different species and opposing interests." It was as if, Eliot wrote, "they were both adrift on one piece of wreck and looked away from each other."

And the gaze turns everywhere, on everything. Nothing is sacrosanct; for those whose innocent artistic taste runs to quaint landscapes and portraits of ordinary people, Eliot describes "that softening influence of the fine arts which makes other people's hardships picturesque." Strong-minded indeed.

One reads such straight-faced ironies with a gradually accumulating sense of danger, as though a hostile gunship had gotten behind one and was shelling the assumptions back in one's interior. Eliot described "the ordinary aping of aristocratic institutions by people who are no more aristocratic than retired grocers." Bang. To most mortals, Eliot wrote, "there is a stupidity which is unendurable and a stupidity which is altogether acceptable—else, indeed, what would become of social bonds?" Blam!

Nor do the shallow escape. Eliot ridicules "the superior power of mystery over fact" in "the general mind" and is devastatingly severe with Rosamond: "Shallow natures dream of an easy sway over the emotions of others, trusting implicitly in their own petty magic to turn the deepest streams, and confident, by pretty gestures and remarks, of making the thing that is not as though it were." Boom!

Eliot does more, however, than smite the Philistines, though they are in a great need of smiting. She also sympathizes profoundly with higher souls who travail and are heavy laden:

Only those who know the supremacy of the intellectual life—the life which has a seed of ennobling thought and purpose within it—can understand the grief of one who falls from that serene activity into the absorbing soul-wasting struggle with worldly annoyances.

In the end we realize that Eliot's scorn of baseness

and pretense manifest no inherent meanness but are protective functions of her deeper love of what is best in humanity. The dejected Lydgate eventually comes under the benevolent eye of Dorothea, and Eliot's prose blooms forth with sudden optimism:

> Lydgate turned, remembering where he was, and saw Dorothea's face looking up at him with a sweet trustful gravity. The presence of a noble nature, generous in its wishes, ardent in its charity, changes the lights for us: we begin to see things again in their larger, quieter masses, and to believe that we too can be seen and judged in the wholeness of our character.

In reading *Middlemarch*, we finally feel that the benevolent Dorothea is the true alter ego of George Eliot, a brilliant writer of noble nature, generous in its wishes and ardent in its charity. And George Eliot, indeed, changes the light for us.

SIX

The Creators

Daniel J. Boorstin

In attempting to discuss Daniel Boorstin's book *The Creators*, one feels like T.S. Eliot's J. Alfred Prufrock, wallowing in an inferno of self-contempt (read "Prufrock" and then read Canto II of Dante's *Inferno* to see how powerfully Eliot laced his lines with Dante's resonant phrases) and muttering, "Do I dare?" and "How should I presume?" and finally, "It is impossible to say just what I mean!"

Well, I am not Lazarus, and I shall not tell you all, but I will tell you a few things. Just as Whitman disclosed the universal in the particular, describing us all by describing himself ("I do not say these things for a dollar, or to fill up time while I wait for a boat," Whitman wrote, "It is you talking just as much as myself....I act as the tongue of you."), Daniel Boorstin has succeeded, by writing "A History of Heroes of the Imagination," in describing the hero in each of our imaginations. Boorstin has found our muse, and the muse is good. Of course, for Philistines, no muse is good muse.

Boorstin, be it recalled, was the Librarian of Congress for twelve years, from 1975 until 1987, after being the director of the National Museum of History and Technology and senior historian of the Smithsonian Institution. He taught history for twenty-five years at the University of Chicago. The author of *The Discoverers* and the three-volume *The Americans* (the third won the

Pulitzer Prize), Boorstin is one of this country's most distinguished scholars.

And yet, in reading between the lines of this beautiful book, one can almost see Boorstin shaking his head in agreement with Nietzsche, who deplored the "dust of the scholars," for Boorstin's heroes are not the colossi of arid scholarship; they are the most human of the human. Boorstin's heroes dared to disturb the universe of tradition and expectation; they were the risk takers, like Abbe Suger, who filled the cathedral of Saint Denis with stained-glass light; like Cervantes, who filled the cathedral of *Don Quixote* with episodes of a crazy old man who always did the right thing (What an idiot!); like the ancient Egyptian architect Imhotep, whose immense Step Pyramid at Saqqara is the world's oldest hewn stone structure (the base is 597 yards wide—think about it); and like the Roman emperor Justinian, who obstinately insisted on marrying the notorious demimondaine Theodora, who then transformed herself into a Christian theologian, and whose equanimity and self-discipline probably saved Justinian's throne.

Beginning with the ancient world, Boorstin moves through the stories—he is a storyteller first of all. We read about the Hindus, Confucius, Buddha, and Greek mythology. There is a chapter each on Moses, Philo of Alexandria (yep, a whole chapter), Saint Augustine, and the *Koran*. Boorstin gives us fascinating chapters on the birth of architecture: megaliths, pyramids, Greek temples, Roman concrete, the domes of the Pantheon and Hagia Sophia, and the beautiful Japanese work with wood. There are chapters on the history of images, in which Boorstin lingers over the Iconoclasts' fear and hatred of images, and chapters on the birth of literature in the ancient world. There are entire sections of *The Creators* on the history of music, the novel, and the Renaissance painters, as well as modern art, music, literature, and architecture. It is an incredible tour, both vast in scope and intimate in feel.

But through all of this survey, it is on the human stories that Boorstin focuses; in the end, we feel we have learned about people. Boorstin has the poet's knack for the telling detail: Mohammed saying that the angels will not enter a house in which there is a picture or a dog (the dogs I know would object); Emerson saying that the barbarians did not arrive in Rome a day too soon; the doomed Boethius resorting to the poetic style of *The Consolation of Philosophy* because he was writing in prison and did not have access to his beloved books; the confident Emperor Trajan building his bridge across the Danube, that his legions might march toward the barbarians, and Hadrian destroying that bridge, that the barbarians might not march toward him; the fact that no Neanderthal burial has ever contained a single bead or piece of bodily decoration; the fact that Dante does not mention his real wife, Gemma, in his writings.

Telling details—the book is filled with them. They are like glimpses into private minds. The black-and-white words of Boorstin's page dissolve into animate color as we read about Boccaccio and Petrarch's convoluted relationship: in all the years of their collaboration and friendship, the bibliophile Petrarch never read his friend Boccaccio's *Decameron*. When the embarrassment became too much, Petrarch finally claimed to have given Boccaccio's book a "hasty perusal," and described it as a "very big volume, written in prose and intended for the masses"—perhaps literary history's most egregious case of damning through faint praise. But then, in their twilight years, Petrarch invited Boccaccio to come and live with him so that they could spend their last days together and combine their libraries, and Boccaccio declined.

Why did Petrarch withhold approval of his friend's masterpiece? Was it jealously? Was he scandalized by the vulgar, ribald character of some of the stories? Was he embarrassed by the unscholarly nature of Boccaccio's book, written in the vernacular Italian instead of Latin? We cannot be sure, but Boorstin protects Boccaccio with subtle irony: "Like other classics of vernacular literature, the *Decameron* was widely read before academic critics dignified it by their attention."

The value of *The Creators* as a text for bright students is manifest; it is a kind of pocket education, introducing students to famous names, epochs in history, a host of gorgeous ideas, and luscious quotations: "The dull mind rises to truth through that which is material," the Abbé Suger stated, and had it inscribed on the bronzed doors of his splendid St. Denis cathedral.

The Creators also contains a vocabulary that is ideally suited for developing thought. In its pages we see words such as *arcane, deified, vicarious, sepulchral, dogma, manifold, festoon, secular, incendiary, autonomous, assuage, retort, megalomaniac, eulogy, threnody, oscillation, edict, variegated, flamboyant, undulating, axiom, misogynist, halcyon, obdurate, decorous, edifying, remunerative, interstices, unctuous, docile, uxorious, shibboleth, salutary, fortuitous, misanthrope, genre, effrontery, erudition, specious, desultory, prosaic, poignant, indolent, patrician, unambiguous, polemics, heterodox, amanuensis, regicide, magnanimous, sanctimonious, redolent, pedantry, paean, archetype, equanimity, histrionic, immured, spurious,* epicure, *ebullience, collusion, boon, leitmotif,* and *expurgated.*

The Creators has vocabulary such as this, Eliot might add, and so much more.

Yet for the teacher of thinking students, Boorstin's *The Creators* has perhaps a higher value, beyond its strength as a source of education. What Boorstin gives us, repeatedly, is insight into the educational experiences of the great creators themselves, and these insights are penetrating.

In the seventh section of *The Creators*, for example, called "The Human Comedy: A Composite Work," Boorstin devotes chapters to Boccaccio, Chaucer, Rabelais, Cervantes, Shakespeare, Milton, Gibbon, Prescott and Parkman, Balzac, and Dickens. The literati sit forward in their minds at the mere mention of these names, and they will not be disappointed. Boorstin's discussions of these authors' works and their place in the history of ideas is excellent, but there is something more: passing like a submarine below the literary surface is a quiet leitmotif on education. From time to time, the surface of the essay is rippled, a periscope pops up, fire one fire two dive dive, little torpedoes bubble toward a rusty assumption, boom, and the leitmotif sinks silently down again, but it is always there. Waiting . . .

For Boccaccio, an illegitimate son, education consisted of learning Latin and accounting and spending six miserable years as an apprentice banker, followed by six years of law school. Eventually, Boccaccio spent time at the royal court of the kings of Naples, but then his father went bankrupt, and he was plunged into disgraced exile in Florence. From this rich mine of personal experience, he produced the *Decameron*.

Chaucer too was born into prosperity. His father was a wine merchant who sent him to a good London school where he learned Latin and French. Like Boccaccio,

Chaucer acquired courtly contacts and a cosmopolitan experience.

Rabelais was the son of a prosperous lawyer and acquired a classical education, learning to read Greek. When that bastion of academe, the Sorbonne, learned that he could read Greek, they seized his Greek books, and Rabelais fled to Montpellier, but there too, he found that the study of Greek was banned:

> Rabelais had impressed his fellows and alarmed his professors by his own translations of the sacred Greek medical texts because a student who could read these texts—and the New Testament—in the original might be tempted to draw his own conclusions.

And we wouldn't want that. As a part of his personal medical study, Rabelais also dissected the corpse of a criminal, something else that was banned by the Sorbonne. Eventually, Rabelais's friend Étienne Dolet published Rabelais's books *Gargantua* and *Pantagruel*—both banned by the Sorbonne—and the unamused Sorbonne burned Dolet at the stake. Dolet took his independence with him into the flames, quipping *"Non dolet ipse Dolet, sed pro ratione dolet"*—Dolet does not suffer for himself, but he suffers for the sake of reason.

We know less about Cervantes than about Rabelais, but we know enough to see that his life would make an extraordinary film. His father was imprisoned, and Cervantes apparently never attended a university but was a voracious bibliophile who devoured every book he could find. He lost his left hand at the Battle of Lepanto, was captured and held for ransom by Algerian pirates, was a slave, was captured trying to escape, was ransomed, jailed for debt, and plunged into poverty, where he eventually wrote dozens of plays that have been lost and his prototype of the novel, the immortal *Don Quixote*. Boorstin notes that Cervantes's education was taken at the School of Hard Knocks.

About Shakespeare we know, if possible, even less, except that he seems to have lacked a university education, but must have been a voracious reader. And strangely, like Mozart, Shakespeare seems to have composed with spontaneous genius, without blots or corrections. We may be forgiven for disregarding Ben Jonson's famous epigram, upon hearing that Shakespeare never blotted out a line: "Would he had blotted a thousand!" As for Shakespeare's status as an academic, Boorstin quotes Coleridge, who was proud to have "demonstrated... that the supposed irregularities and extravagances of Shakespeare were the mere dreams of a pedantry that arraigned the eagle because it had not the dimensions of a swan." No swan himself, Coleridge scoffed that "on the Continent the works of Shakespeare are honoured in a double way; by the admiration of Italy and Germany, and by the contempt of the French."

Boccaccio, Chaucer, Rabelais, Cervantes, and Shakespeare: in none of these writers do we see formal education as the cause of their famous effects. In fact, we begin to see a trend of minds emerging in spite of, rather than as a result of, formal education. We see lives lived vividly, vast quantities of books read voraciously, independence and even defiance of tradition and authority, and for one reason or another, time. Some writers had independent wealth to give them the leisure to read and think, others had prison, but one way or another, each writer found time.

In the case of Milton, we see these factors at work. Milton was born in London to a comfortable life.

His father, Milton later wrote, "destined me in early childhood for the study of literature." Milton went to St. Paul's school where he learned Latin, Greek, and Hebrew. His father hired tutors to teach the boy more foreign languages at home. Milton received bachelor's and master's degrees from Cambridge University, but he found it "disgusting to be constantly subjected to the threats of a rough tutor and to other indignities which my spirit cannot endure." At Cambridge, he was whipped. After leaving Cambridge, Milton, who would become totally blind, needed time to recoup. He spent six years at home in Hammersmith reading the Greek and Latin writers "to repair the pedantries of Cambridge." Having been a "voracious, round-the-clock reader from the age of twelve," Milton would later write in *Areopagitica*, his defense of freedom of the press, that "books are not absolutely dead things, but...do preserve as in a vial the purest efficacy and extraction of that living intellect that bred them." In the end, Milton's paradise was lost; his defense of freedom sent him into hiding, but he was captured and imprisoned, and his books were burned.

Edward Gibbon was also born to wealth. His father was a member of Parliament, and he was a sickly child who withdrew into the world of books after his mother died. He spent two years at Westminster School, but left for private tutors because of his ill health. Gibbon remembered that he:

> ...secretly rejoiced in those infirmities, which delivered me from the exercises of the school and the society of my equals. As often as I was tolerably exempt from danger and pain, reading, free desultory reading, was the employment and comfort of my solitary hours

Gibbon went to Oxford, where his fourteen months were "the most idle and unprofitable of my whole life." Gibbon mastered Latin, Greek, and French, and embarked on a personal program of study: "reviewing the Latin Classics under the four divisions of 1 Historians, 2 Poets, 3 Orators, and 4 Philosophers in a chronological series from the days of Plautus and Sallust to the decline of the language and Empire of Rome." That was in his leisure time in Switzerland. When he returned to England, he "continued his wide reading for another five years." In a visit to Rome, Gibbon got the idea to write the story of the city's decline, and the rest is history. Distrusting abstractions, he took twenty years of his life to tell the stories of the Romans, and he brought the lives, not the generalizations, to the fore. The result, Boorstin says, is the "most read and most readable work of a modern historian."

William Hickling Prescott was born to a wealthy family in Boston. He went to Harvard where he accomplished little and where he was blinded in the left eye by a crust of bread in a food fight in the Commons. Two years later, he lost the vision in his right eye. Another voracious reader, Prescott had to be read to for the rest of his life. Family members and employees did the reading, and he dictated notes that were read back to him. When the nearly blind Prescott finally began his *Conquest of Mexico*, he had to supplement his personal library of five thousand volumes with abundant manuscripts that a former Harvard classmate sent to him from Spain. Prescott had some of them read to him twelve times. He spent the rest of his life listening to books and dictating his own, listening through his dim flicker of vision and creating, Boorstin says, masterpieces out of his "miraculous memory."

Prescott's fellow American, Francis Parkman, was also a New England Brahmin who could afford books and time. Like Gibbon, Parkman was sickly. Sent to live with his grandfather, he "walked twice a day to a school of high but undeserved reputation, in the town of Medford. Here I learned very little, and spent the intervals of schooling more profitably in collecting eggs, insects, and reptiles...." He entered Harvard, studied Latin and Greek, and spent time hiking and camping, where strenuous experiences out of doors left him with numerous physical ailments. Parkman traveled to Europe, went to Harvard Law School, and went west, where he saw Indians and wild lands. When he returned to Boston, his eyesight became so bad that he had to dictate *The Oregon Trail* as friends and family members read his notes to him. Parkman's works, like Prescott's and Gibbon's, were achievements of humanity. Boorstin wryly observes:

> Never professionally "trained" as a historian, he never lost the enthusiasm of the amateur. And he wrote before the rise of academic history would make readability suspect.

When Honoré de Balzac was born, his mother sent him off to a wet nurse for three years, and then when he was four, he was sent to the College de Vendome. The school honored no holidays, and Honoré's mother came to see him twice in six years. Later, Honoré studied at the Lycée Charlemagne, as Boorstin says, "without distinction." He then studied law at the Sorbonne, but in spite of his family's expectations:

...he never found the lawyers' ways of thought congenial, and his whimsies made him a menace in the staid chambers. "Monsieur Balzac is requested not to come today," the head clerk once wrote him, "because there is a great deal of work to be done."

Balzac left this behind, and with modest support from his mother, he went off to Paris to become a writer. His embarrassed parents told the neighbors that Balzac had gone to live with a cousin. By the age of thirty-four, he had published two dozen novels and had found his life's work: to write a vast multinovel mosaic with reappearing characters and a new literary form—the novel of ideas. Balzac's endless proof corrections exasperated his publishers, but he was undeterred. "Salute me," he wrote to his sister, "I am on the way to becoming a genius!"

Dickens's pitiful early life is better known. His father was a loving parent who could not live within his income and was imprisoned in Marshalsea Debtor's Prison, where Charles's mother actually went to live with her husband. Charles and his sister spent Sundays there. Poverty forced his parents to take Charles out of school. When he was sixteen, Charles got a job as court reporter in the Consistory Court of the Bishop of London, "where he acquired a treasury of jargon, obfuscation, and legal muddles for any number of novels. At eighteen he secured a reader's ticket at the British Museum and he read fervently in his spare hours." Without quitting his day job, he began writing, and at the age of twenty-five, he was a literary sensation, famous in a way that, as Boorstin notes, "is still not easy to explain." Part of Dickens's popularity may have been due to his democratic views. Boorstin describes him as a Victorian *populis* and adds that when Dickens went to America:

...he had been lionized by readers, and formed warm personal friendships with Longfellow and others, but he was vilified by the press. Slavery in America, which Dickens loudly opposed, they said was none of his business. His plea for an American copyright law to protect authors from pirating they called purely mercenary, a motive that Americans found suspect in foreigners.

For the average reader (as though there were one) the lives of these gifted writers might be simply fascinating, but the striking educational fact about them is the absence of education as a positive influence in their lives. Over and again, formal education either is nonexistent or else it is present as a pernicious experience that must be "repaired" by years of personal reading and self-education.

In fact, intense, self-directed self-education is what emerges as the largest single factor in the development of these writers. Boccaccio learned more at the royal court than at law school. Chaucer immersed himself in court life and travel. Rabelais struggled against the Sorbonne, which not only did not encourage him but banned the study of Greek, seized his Greek books, and banned his own books. Cervantes had a limited education but was a voracious reader who led an adventurous life. Like Cervantes, Shakespeare apparently never attended a university, but his towering vocabulary shows him to have been a vast reader. Milton attended Cambridge and was so scarred by the experience that he spent six years of private reading to repair its pedantries. Gibbon rejoiced that he had left the exercises of school behind at an early age so that he could embark on a life of free desultory reading. Prescott was an undistinguished student at Harvard but devoured his personal library of five thousand volumes and, after losing his sight, had innumerable works read aloud to him, many of them repeatedly. Parkman learned "very little" at school but was another voracious reader who had to be read to by friends and family. Balzac left his unsatisfying educational experience behind and set out to become a writer, and Dickens had little formal education to speak of but grew up in a tempest of human emotions that he would never forget. He got himself a reader's ticket to the library.

In each case we see a formal education contrasted with a personal education. In each case it is the personal education that appears to have been most significant; the formal education seems to have been ineffectual or worse.

When we look at the common elements of the personal educations of these writers, we see the vital importance of choice, of self-direction, of freedom to concentrate extraordinary amounts of time on intense personal fascinations (Gibbon the Romans, Prescott the history of Mexico, Parkman the West), of vast amounts of time to read, and read, and read. We see the importance of books—real books, not age-graded (degraded) textbooks. We the importance of an individualized program that fits the student both intellectually and in lifestyle. We see the importance of foreign language study: most of these writers were accomplished polyglots whose minds were enlarged by the cross-fertilization of words, literatures, and cultures—possibly the one area where formal education was a benefit, but even there, these writers notably directed themselves far beyond the assignments of a formal foreign language program.

Perhaps the word that comes most to mind, as we reflect

on these writers' educations, is *self*. Each writer was able to use learning as a springboard for self-authentication. He was not circumscribed by an institutional structure in which being himself was suppressed, or opposed, or postponed. He was not required to lose his day passively obeying the monotonous authority at the front, and his entire night completing tedious textbook assignments.

By discovering themselves through self-directed learning, these gifted writers became heroes of the imagination. There is a message here, if philosophy could find it out.

SEVEN

Gulliver's Travels

Jonathan Swift

A 1996 television production of Jonathan Swift's *Gulliver's Travels* renewed our appreciation of this hilarious, stinging, classic satire. Regarded and read as a children's book of fantastic adventures to the lands of pipsqueaks and giants, *Gulliver's Travels* also bridges the generations and satisfies the most advanced intellects; it is the greatest—and surely the fiercest—satire in the English language.

Born in Ireland in 1667, Swift rose to become dean of St. Patrick's Cathedral in Dublin. Like many another famous intellect, Swift had an undistinguished academic record, graduating from Trinity College, Dublin, with a B.A. degree *speciali gratia*—by special grace, but Swift soon developed the razor-sharp prose style and satiric edge that made him famous in *Gulliver's Travels, A Modest Proposal*, and other works.

For readers of many ages in our century, in recent centuries, and in future centuries, *Gulliver's Travels* is a special reading and learning experience. Like *Treasure Island* and *Peter Pan, Gulliver's Travels* can be read not only by educated adults but by young readers who will love the adventures in Lilliput and Brobdingnag and who will discover an exotic tale of *Robinson Crusoe*-like adventure. Gulliver's experiences with the high-flying thinkers of Laputa and with the foul yahoos of Houyhnhnm land are memorable fantasies for imaginative children.

And for strengthening the mind, *Gulliver's Travels* offers an element of academic rigor shared by other outstanding children's classics (Kenneth Grahame's *The Wind in the Willows* is a particularly good example)— namely, challenging vocabulary.

In reading *Gulliver's Travels*, students will encounter words such as *manifest, copious, repartee, comely, austere, tedious, maxim, menial, encomium, circumspect, ignominy, expostulate, soporific, declivity, schism, acute, viscous, vindicate, concupiscence, countenance, intrepid, auspicious, profound, buffoon, visage, avarice, erudite,* and *odious.*

They will encounter main-line classic words such as *venerate* and *sagacity,* and they will also encounter more unusual but satisfying words such as *noisome, pillory, ructation,* and *obeisance.*

Students will read Swift's amazing story and absorb with it a vocabulary course in context. They will read that Gulliver was *inured* to hardship, that he drank a *soporiferous* medicine, that he lay in a *profound* sleep, and that he thought of a best *expedient.* They will find that he stood like a *colossus,* that the Lilliputians regarded him as a *prodigious* person, and that he walked with the utmost *circumspection* to avoid treading on Lilliputians.

On and on the sentences flow, lucid and wondrous, flecked with words, and words, and words. There are hundreds of good words. Adjectives, for example: the Emperor of Lilliput is *puissant.* The enemy is *potent.* The dominions are *celestial.* And the Majesty is *sublime.* The diminutive mortals are *intrepid.* The disposition is *melancholy,* The reign is *auspicious.* And the behavior is *discreet.* There is a *lucid* substance, a *menial* office, an *insatiable* desire of seeing foreign countries, a *staunch* ship, a fear of being *censured* as *tedious*, and an *austere countenance*. The adjectives swarm around the story: *august, austere, rustic, vulgar, comely, acute, officious, erudite, odious, pernicious*, and *pecuniary*. There is a wistful *melancholy*, a *magnanimous* prince, a *florid* style, and a *glutinous* matter. There is an *ebullient* humor.

Meanwhile, diminutive pipsqueaks are crawling over Gulliver's stomach, and giants are putting him in their pocket.

In doing so, they generate verbs. Gulliver *entreats* his Majesty. The philosophers *conjecture*. The Lilliputians *forbear*, and the emperors of Blefuscu *expostulate*. A wall *encompasses*, and a species *propagates*. Censure is *incurred*. Information is *procured*. A sail is *descried*. A victim is *cashiered*. Gulliver *ingratiates* himself and relates facts that *redound* to the honor of his country. Gulliver's foolish ideas are *imputed* to a disorder in his brain. Grievances are *redressed*, people are *apprised*, and *exploits* in war are *ascribed* to cowards. Masters *interpose*. Corruptions *aggravate*. Human understanding *debases*.

Of course, these verbs need nouns; that is the deal that grammar makes with our minds. And Jonathan Swift did not lack, it is clear, for nouns. Nouns poured from his pen in copious profusion. Gulliver wears a *jerkin*, descends a *declivity*, thinks of an *expedient*, has a smattering of *lingua franca*, takes out a *scimitar*, views a *palisade*, and is accused of making a *schism*. The Lilliputians tie Gulliver with *ligatures*, sling up *hogsheads*, follow in *retinues*, and lodge Gulliver in an *edifice*. In *Gulliver's Travels* there are *factions, fortnights, animosities*, and *juntos*. There is an *embargo* laid by the Emperor, and the prince receives Gulliver with all possible *encomiums*. There is a *maxim* that Gulliver never sees put in practice.

There are *rudiments* of *docility* that people are supposed to have. Three hundred cooks prepare Gulliver's *victuals*. There is a sour *countenance* and a great *alacrity*. Gulliver consults with a *cabal*, crumbles bread on a *trencher*, resolves in a dangerous *juncture*, and frightens an *urchin* with roaring. The Captain falls sick of an *ague*. A giant virtuoso thinks that Gulliver might be an *embryo*. In the mouths of court pages, there are the usual *repartees*. The head is decapitated from a *malefactor*. There is a contemptible *varlet*. There are venerable *sages*. Gulliver makes an admirable *panegyric* upon his country. In Lorbrulgrud, the crew and passengers are brought in a *tumbril*, and a worthy gentleman has some tincture of learning.

There is *raillery*, and a *zenith*, and *effluvia*, and a *lodestone*. There is a *rhomboid*. And a *hautboy*. And a *zodiac*. There are many other wild, impossible *chimeras*.

Gulliver sees a *repository* of water, and an *affliction* of *dearth*, and a profound *obeisance*.

Amidst storms, and waves, and giants, and talking horses, and vile yahoos, and flying islands, and diminutive Lilliputians, the words pour forth. We find *anagram, lineament, acrostic, quantum, apothecary, and petulance*. There is *purulent*, and *fetid*, and *scrofulous*, and *palatable*. Characters are *restive*, and *sublime*, and *singular*, and *sallow*. Happiness is *sublunary*.

My edition of *Gulliver's Travels* is 355 pages long and averages 300 words to the page. In these 106,000 words, students will experience a burst of intellectual growth that is difficult to equal in less challenging books. On one page alone, I see *felicity, patrimony, judicature, bulwark, degenerate, sanctity, erudition, fidelity, sovereign, dominion*, and *posterity*.

And as if this rigorous use of English diction were

not enough, this children's book is dense with satirical challenges to authority and custom, enough to help anyone learn to think:

> It is a maxim among these lawyers, that whatever has been done before may legally be done again; and therefore they take special care to record all the decisions formerly made against common justice and the general reason of mankind. These, under the name of precedents, they produce as authorities, to justify the most iniquitous opinions; and the judges never fail of directing accordingly.

Although *Gulliver's Travels* in its unabridged form is too difficult and too mature in content for young elementary children, it is a priceless asset for the education of thinking middle school and high school students ready for a writer who suffered no fool or foolishness gladly.

EIGHT

Crime and Punishment

Fyodor Dostoevsky

It had to happen.

In the history of the novel as an art form, someone had to turn away from gregarious stories about relationships between individuals and write a story about the relationship between an individual and himself.

It was Dostoyevsky who turned the scope around and peered into the interior.

Dostoyevsky.

That introvert.

But then, Dostoyevsky paid for his introversion the old-fashioned way. He earned it.

Awakened by Czar Nicholas's police and arrested with fifteen of his associates for subversive thinking, Dostoyevsky was sentenced to be shot. It was 1849, and he was only twenty-eight. The gang of fifteen were taken to a platform in Semenov Square, preached to, wrapped alive in burial shrouds, and tied to posts.

Ready, aim . . .

Up came the rifles.

In came the courier: "Wait!"

It seems the czar had commuted the sentences to hard labor in Siberia. And had planned to all along. But first, why not have a little sadistic fun.

Oh, Nicholas I, you funny guy.

In Dostoyevsky's four years of labor in Siberia, he had time to think. Ostracized by the other prisoners because he was born of noble blood and probably because he was isolated by his unusual powers of thought and imagination, he had time to think. He had time to read; he was permitted one book: *The New Testament.*

In the end he thought not about death, but about life, life through Christ. Dostoyevsky wrote, "I...believe that there is nothing more beautiful, more profound, more sympathetic, more reasonable, more manly, and more perfect than Christ. Furthermore, if anyone proved to me that Christ was outside the truth, and it really was a fact that the truth was outside of Christ, I would rather remain with Christ than with the truth." And so this young Russian genius who had suffered much had come to believe that our lives are redeemed through suffering, as Christ suffered.

Suffering? What a goal. Not very snappy. Hard to sell that to the masses. Not the stuff of hedonistic Ad Street jingles. Sounds un-American. And of course, it is. Daniel Boorstin writes that Dostoyevsky "laid siege to the values of the West" but ironically became an idol of Western literature anyway. Yes, the desirability of suffering is not exactly what drives our national energies.

After four years in prison, Dostoyevsky had to spend six years in the army and was finally released in 1859. Although they seem to have lived in different centuries, Dostoyevsky wrote *Crime and Punishment* during Lincoln's presidency and finished it in 1865, the year of Lincoln's assassination. It is a strange 19th century juxtaposition: Lincoln, the Emancipator, elevating Jefferson's 18th century concepts to a mantra, and Dostoyevsky, the creator, prefiguring the inward torments and anxieties of 20th century existentialism.

Dostoyevsky reads more like Camus than like his contemporary, Charles Dickens (1812-1870).

Dostoyevsky led the way for modern literature's expedition into the self. He was the scout, the pathfinder.

Crime and Punishment is a haunting, beautiful book. The story of Raskolnikov, an ax-murderer who wanders as a dead soul through the shadows of himself and is redeemed through the love of a skinny harlot, *Crime and Punishment* is an epic of triumph, of gloom illuminated, of hope and life. It is the story of a modern Lazarus, come forth from the dead.

Regardless of the depths of your degradation, *Crime and Punishment* tells us, you need not be degraded always. You can make it back. Lost soul, come forth.

An essential work in the education of anyone who wishes to know literature's highest accomplishments (*The Brothers Karamazov* is regarded as Dostoyevsky's greatest novel), *Crime and Punishment* also has characteristics that make it highly appropriate in the education of intellectually motivated students. It is complex and challenging, it is among the most profound works of literature, it is introspective and metacognitive, it focuses on moral growth, it contains numerous unforgettable characters, it is a landmark in the history of the novel, it displays an extraordinary use of symbolism and other artistic devices, and not least of its advantages, it contains a strong vocabulary.

In the Signet Classic edition, translated by Sidney Monas, the vocabulary is a veritable SAT prep course. Assuming an aggressive approach to the vocabulary by students and teacher, the students will gain ground against a stratum of diction that includes *abject, acute, prevaricate, fastidious, palpable, denizen, sonorous, elicit, magnanimous, imbue, dissipate, bravado, wizened, bilious, monomaniac, casuistry, implacable, sultry, profound, capricious, thrall, sequester, efface, grotesque, abyss, esthetic, ineffable, amiable, morose, pondering, disheveled, perplexity, querulous, sallow, languid, malevolent, disseminate, platitude, irrevocable, premasticated, condescending, pensive, resonant, desperado, resolute, sententious, wistful, irascible, unction, peremptory, wan, nonplused, eccentric, acme, serene, cloying, sedate, diffidence, paroxysm, pro forma, abase, incipient, avid, furtive, piqued, crestfallen, lackey, sardonic, plaintive, despotism, egotist, commensurate, retrograde, phalanstery, felicitous, obtrusive, brazen, fetid, tangential, assuage, ambiguous, beneficent, banality, dyspeptic, dissipation, affront, flagrant, ephemeral, chronic, caustic, captious, retort, wry, allude, baleful, destitute, venerate, incredulous, supplication, dejection, degradation, fortuitous, manifestation, stupefying, censure, askance, odious, reiteration, enigmatic, oblique, vacuous, buffoon, gratis, limpid, insidious, solicitude, gambit, denouement, sojourn, omniscient, nihilist, scrofulous, motley, vulgarian, countenance, lorgnette, dissonance, plenary, hauteur, provincial, portentous, quailed, deign, anecdote, proliferate, pandemonium, patronymic, milksop, benefactor, forensic, stupor, pernicious, catechism, bated, urchin, superfluous, self-abnegation, distended, pallid, respite, plausible, bourgeois, sophistry, tedious, idiom, debauchee, a priori, subjugation, voluptuary, somber, grimace, ardent, sumptuous, scullion, venal, mufti, appurtenance, garrulous, dissolute, incoherent, enumerate, privation, inculpate, assiduous, mitigate, taciturn, fervid,* and *burnoose.*

Many of these words are used many times in *Crime and Punishment*, and they span the range from the often-known, to the somewhat-known, to the little-known. Most students will have an accurate sense of words such as *oblique, abject, resolute,* and *eccentric.* The better readers will know words such as *odious, enigmatic, pandemonium,* and *incredulous.* But few students will know words such as *garrulous, venal, sophistry, casuistry,* and *ineffable.* Teachers who plan to use the Monas translation of *Crime and Punishment* would be rewarded by teaching and discussing this list in advance of the reading, allowing students to find and understand the words in context as they go.

On the basis of its powerful vocabulary alone, we would be tempted to include *Crime and Punishment* in a curriculum for bright students, but, of course, vocabulary is only the beginning of the intellectual benefits the book possesses. Another is an exceptionally brilliant use of symbols, woven through the book as a continuous tapestry. Yet, although the book is polished like a symbolic jewel and is everywhere replete with symbols that lift the meaning to the mind, Dostoyevsky is so adept at using these symbols that the casual reader might miss them utterly. It is not uncommon for students to read chapter after chapter, loaded with repeated symbols and remain oblivious, completely unaware of their presence. *Crime and Punishment* is therefore a rare opportunity for the teacher of literature to reveal to students why and how novelists use symbols to enhance the power and meaning of their novels.

There are numerous examples of symbols in *Crime and Punishment* that we could discuss, but perhaps the easiest one to survey is Dostoyevsky's use of the number three. Three, being the symbol of the Holy Trinity, of the three-person God of the Bible, represents for Christians the greatest presence in the universe, the present omnipresence of God the Father, Son, and Holy Ghost. And Dostoyevsky omits no opportunity to permeate his novel of resurrection with the holy number three. His characters move through hosts of threes, are surrounded by threes, experience threes everywhere they turn. Through its numerical symbol, the Trinity is present everywhere in the book, whether the characters—or readers—realize it or not. Three is used so many times in *Crime and Punishment* that it strains credulity, and yet many readers will never notice it, so distracting is Dostoyevsky's plot, and so delicate is his style.

Lest this seem exaggerated, consider some examples of threes that Dostoyevsky embeds in his story without ever calling direct attention to them. Although the list of threes is long, a patient list will show, in a way that mere saying so never would, just how pervasive is Dostoyevsky's use of the number three as a symbol. In *Crime and Punishment*, one key is three times as big as the others, there are three small children in a remote and barbarous province, the kids have not seen a crust of bread for three days, Raskolnikov's room has three old chairs, the mailman is paid three kopecks, three years and she's a human wreck, three kopecks go to Nastasia for a letter, Raskolnikov eats three spoonfuls without appetite, Razumikhin buys Raskolnikov three shirts, Raskolnikov stands beside three people in an audience, Raskolnikov fishes three five-kopeck coins out of his pocket, he says he would leave town for maybe three years, he pulls the bell three times, a driver yells three times for Marmeladov to get out of the way of the horses, Razumikhin tells Raskolnikov that he is three times as smart as Zosimov, Razumikhin tells Zosimov that after another three years he will not be getting up for his patients any more, there is a legacy of a triple-damned yesterday, people have been separated for three years, there are another three days, three months ago, three years, three chairs, a stranger glances at all three characters, Dunia goes to the third floor, Raskolnikov says that in the third place..., he goes to the third floor in his dream, Martha Petrovna is forced to sit home for the third day, Svidrigailov uses a switch for the third time, he is bored for three days, he is lounging around for three days, he has been in St. Petersburg for three days, he was bought out for thirty thousand, Martha Petrovna has come for three times now, Svidrigailov is wide awake three times, Martha Petrovna leaves Dunia three thousand rubles in her will, Dunia can get the money in three weeks, Razumikhin finds that publishing three works would bring in a hundred rubles per book, Sonia lives in a house of three stories, a door opens three steps away, a wall has three windows facing the canal embankment, Raskolnikov thinks there are three possibilities for Sonia, Sonia stands three steps from the table, Raskolnikov expects to be on the road to prison in three weeks, Porfiry asks whether a third man could be considered guilty, an artisan comes back a third time, the Terebiev girl is about to take on her third liberal marriage, Sonia sits down for the third time, there are three hundred-ruble bills on the table, Sonia gets up from the table three times during the conversation, someone knocks at the door three times, Svidrigailov places three orphans in establishments, Raskolnikov feels calmer than he had for three days, Razumikhin has been to Raskolnikov's three times, Raskolnikov is wolfing down boiled beef as if he had not eaten for three days, three is a crowd, sometimes nobody talks to Svidrigailov for three days, there is a third party, Raskolnikov imagines three thousand rubles, Svidrigailov offers to get Raskolnikov a ticket in three days, he stands at the window for three minutes longer, he has a small three-shot revolver, there is a three-year-old fir tree, there are three bushes, there are three five-percent bonds, the bonds come to a value of three thousand, there is a promised bride on the third block of Vasilievsky Island, Raskolnikov's mother reads his article for the third time, Gunpowder emerges from the third room, there are three hundred and seventeen silver rubles, there are three twenty-kopeck pieces, there is a project of spending three years acquiring the basis of a fortune, the tramps have seen a cold spring in the wilderness three years ago, and only three workers are sent.

Three: God, God, and God.

Having challenged your patience with examples of the number three—thank you—I will not test it again with the color yellow. But I could.

The color yellow represents sickness, especially moral sickness, Christian sickness. As you might guess, *Crime and Punishment* is filled with yellow. Everything is yellow: wallpaper, furniture, wood...okay, will stop. Just promise you will believe me. And this sick color accompanies a host of direct references to sickness, to mental illness, which Dostoyevsky reveals as a kind of theological illness. It is not really Raskolnikov's body that is yellow and sick; it is his soul. Infatuated with his own gifted mind and his respect for the powerful will of Napoleon, he has turned his heart to logic, and he has turned his back on God. In the end, on the last page of the book, life, divine Life, replaces logic, and the murderer Raskolnikov is resurrected. He is a modern Lazarus brought back from the dead.

Perhaps the most powerful symbol in *Crime and Punishment* is the symbol of the threshold. Used so subtly that it resists detection, the symbol of the threshold fills the pages of the novel. It takes a variety of forms. Often, it is the threshold of a door, and a character will stand at the threshold, pondering whether to enter or not. Sometimes two characters stand on either side of the threshold and listen to each other listening. Sometimes a character will wait silently on the other side of a threshold and eavesdrop. In *Crime and Punishment*, bridges are thresholds, and characters stop in the middle of the bridge, deciding which side to go to.

Deciding, see? That is the point.

Crime and Punishment is an extended metaphor for choice, moral choice, spiritual choice. And every decision is a choice, a threshold, a midpoint on a bridge. Should I go this way or that way? At one point Raskolnikovcrosses the Nikolaevsky Bridge over the Neva River. Without realizing it, he is walking straight down the middle (get it?), and he is struck across the back with a whip by a carriage driver. People laugh, and a woman thrusts money into his hand. "Take it, my dear man," she says,"for Christ's joy." Raskolnikov pauses:

> He...turned to the Neva, facing in the direction of the palace. There was not a cloud in the sky, and the water was almost blue, a rarity for the Neva. The dome of the cathedral, which cannot be seen to better advantage than from this bridge twenty paces from the chapel, glittered marvelously, and through the clear air its every ornament could be seen in vivid detail.

Decision time. What should he do with the money given for Christ's love? Should he go to the church side of the bridge, or to the other side? He throws the coin into the river and goes home, away from the cathedral.

Dostoyevsky writes, "He felt as though he had cut himself off at that moment, with a scissors as it were, from everything and everyone."

And he had.

Sometimes the contrast between two characters represents a threshold. Sonia, with her absolute faith in God, her constantly emphasized "childlike" innocence, and her unconditional love of Raskolnikov, is contrasted with Svidrigailov, the voluptuary, the libertine, the amoral cynic. As if on a bridge between two directions, Raskolnikov stands between Sonia and Svidrigailov, horrified by the moral reproach of Sonia's love of God, and horrified by the repulsive iciness of Svidrigailov's depraved godlessness. Which direction should Raskolnikov take: "Sonia represented an implacable verdict, an irreversible decision. It was either her way or Svidrigailov's."

Either/or.

This element in the novel, this emphasis on the nature of moral decision (*de*, down; *cise*, cut; *ion*, act), makes *Crime and Punishment* an important book for teachers of bright students, who tend to have exceptional interest in moral questions.

In explaining his murders, to himself and to others, Raskolnikov uses the word *transgress*. He wants to be able to transgress the limits that restrict ordinary human beings. Viewing these limits as both social/external and personal/internal, Raskolnikov compares himself to Napoleon, whom he sees as strong and free, able to define his own rules, able to orchestrate the deaths of thousands of human beings in the service of a greater cause, able to overcome any personal pangs of wrongdoing. Napoleon, Raskolnikov feels, was able to cross the lines that stop lesser mortals, to choose actions forbidden by traditional religious instruction. This terrible and specious logic, which permits superior individuals to disregard external codes of conscience if their own internal thinking finds their decisions to support a higher purpose, is attractive to Raskolnikov. It is a threshold that he feels bound to cross himself if he is to consider himself a superior being. Being able to dare to transgress, to cross the threshold into individual definition of moral law, is the real goal of his murder. Though he takes valuables from the murder scene, he never makes use of them. The act of transgressing, of crossing the threshold into moral self-legislation, is the goal.

In the end, Raskolnikov's plan falls through. Denying that he feels remorse but constantly tormented by a profound need to confess, he follows the advice of Sonia, Porfiry (the Colombo-like detective who knows from the beginning that Raskolnikov is guilty), and Svidrigailov and turns himself in. He is convicted and sent to Siberia, where Sonia follows him. It is only there, after years of suffering, that he is finally redeemed and begins to feel both remorse for his crime and love for Sonia. In the end, Dostoyevsky writes, "Life replaced logic, and in his consciousness something quite different now had to elaborate and articulate itself."

Life replaced logic.

If there is a more important message for our century, or a more important model of the world for students to discuss, one wonders what it could be. It is not just that life-replaced-logic summarizes modern morality plays such as *Star Wars*, where the life of the Force guides Luke Skywalker against the darthy logic of the Dark Side; it is that a life/logic dichotomy stands behind many of history's actual events. The Nazis used their dark logic and efficiency to perpetrate a war on the world and a holocaust on millions of innocent people. Having a problem with part of your population? One logical possibility for solving that problem is to rid the world of that population. Ergo, there will be no more trouble from that group.

Logic.

A double-edged sword.

What *Crime and Punishment* gives us is a profound examination of the failure of inhuman, soulless, godless logic. It shows us that logic must operate within the needs and values of life and that when this balance is upset, the result is ax murder—or worse.

And there is this: it is a powerful testament to Dostoyevsky's depth that for Raskolnikov's horrid crime, his worst punishment was internal.

NINE

The Lives of the Artists

Vasari

He knew Michelangelo. Giorgio Vasari knew Michelangelo. He observed many of Michelangelo's works in progress and saw the world's first awed reaction to the bright new Sistine Chapel ceiling. Vasari and Michelangelo were friends; they wrote letters to each other when they were apart. And Vasari himself, though he is remembered more for his book, was a popular Renaissance painter in his own right, an artist. He knew about these things.

Imagine that a book were suddenly discovered containing elaborate personal recollections and biographical information on, say, John the Baptist. Or Archimedes. Or Alexander. Or Joan of Arc. Well, *Lives of the Artists* is a book by a fellow artist who was the friend, student, and confidant of Michelangelo Buonarroti. Perhaps that accounts for Vasari's Michelangelo chapter being far longer than any other in the book—one hundred and twenty pages compared to only forty pages for the chapter on Raphael. As though space devoted to Michelangelo's work needed justification.

Vasari's personal knowledge of Michelangelo alone, even if the book possessed no other merit, would give it a special place in intellectual history, for Michelangelo may have been the most gifted artist to have worked in this world. The accomplishments of alien artists in distant worlds have yet to be compared.

But the book does possess other merits. In its complete form, Vasari's *Lives* contains biographies of a hundred and sixty artists; in the Penguin Classic edition, translator George Bull selects twenty of the greatest artists, names that are still ascendant in the 20th century: Cimabue and Giotto, Ghiberti, Massaccio, Alberti, Uccelo, Brunelleschi and his friend Donatello, Fra Angelico and Fra Filippo Lippi, Botticelli and Verocchio. Pierro della Francesca. Mantegna. Giorgione and Correggio. Verrocchio, Leonardo da Vinci, Raphael, and Michelangelo.

Of course, Vasari did not know all of these artists personally. He was born in 1511 when Michelangelo was already thirty-six and died ten years after Michelangelo in 1574. Giotto (pronounced JOT-oh), on the other hand, died in 1337. Brunelleschi, who built the dome for Florence's cathedral, died in 1446. Donatello in 1466. But even though these artists had worked and died long before Vasari wrote their lives, their works were still fresh, intact, and most importantly, extant when he did his research. He was able to travel through Italy and to see, sketch, describe, and even collect paintings and drawings that have since been lost. Works of art that in the four centuries since Vasari's lifetime have been misplaced, destroyed, effaced, burned, or even blown up in world wars were still proud community possessions in 1550, and through his descriptions we can visit the Italy of the Renaissance where paintings, drawings, sculpture, and architecture had a fab popular profile that in the 20th century is equaled only—perhaps—by the modern media of film and television, although it seems somehow amiss to describe Michelangelo as the Tom Cruise of Renaissance Italy. Surely, no one ever described Michelangelo as Top Brush.

Most of us will approach Vasari's unique book with differing knowledge about different artists. We may perhaps be better informed about Giotto than about Uccelo, more knowledgeable about Donatello than about Mantegna. But taken as a group, Vasari's artists are the transcendent artists of the Italian Renaissance, and their names have entered the vocabulary of the world. Even little children must be suffered to speak unto us the names of the Ninja Turtles: Leonardo, Donatello, Raphael, and Michelangelo.

As we read our way through Vasari's short biographies, there are numerous qualities that rise to our attention. One is that although Vasari does, almost tediously at times, list and describe the known works of his artists in elaborate technical detail, expecting us to share his enthusiasm for color, line, design, composition, and fidelity, he also departs from mere cataloging to give us dazzling anecdotes about the artists' lives and personalities.

Take Giotto, please. Giotto was a 13th century (1266-1337) Florentine painter, sculptor, and architect who is believed to have resurrected art from its death at the hands of the barbarians. Vasari explains that painters owe to Giotto the same debt they owe to nature because:

> For after the many years during which the methods and outlines of good painting had been buried under the ruins caused by war it was Giotto alone who, by God's favour, rescued and restored the art, even though he was born among incompetent artists.

Vasari tells the story of how Cimabue was traveling from Florence to Vespignano and saw the ten-year-old Giotto tending sheep by the side of the road, entertaining himself by scratching a drawing of a sheep with a pointed stone on a smooth rock. Cimabue was so impressed with the boy's talent that he asked Giotto's father for permission to take the boy back with him to Florence, where he taught him to paint. There, like many a good pupil, Giotto surpassed his master.

Once, years later, a courtier from Pope Benedict IX came to see Giotto and asked him for a sample painting to show his holiness, that his holiness might choose to commission a work. Giotto looked at the courtier, took out a sheet of paper and a brush dipped in red, and drew a perfect circle with a twist of his hand.

> Then, with a smile, he said to the courtier: "There's your drawing."
> As if he were being ridiculed, the courtier replied: "Is this the only drawing I'm to have?"
> "It's more than enough," answered Giotto. "Send it along with the others and you'll see whether it's understood or not."

You can guess: the Pope understood the circle on the paper, and Giotto got the commission.

Giotto was fearless and loved a joke. When the king of Naples told Giotto that he wanted to make him the first man of Naples, "Giotto retorted that he was already the first man in Naples, since he was living at the very gates of the city by the Porta Reale." Another time, the king told Giotto that it was so hot, he would quit painting for a while, "If I were you." Giotto replied, "And so would I, if I were you." He continued painting.

And then, Vasari tells this Giotto story, surely one of the most charming in all of art history:

There is a story that when Giotto was still a young man in Cimabue's workshop, he once painted on the nose of one of the figures Cimabue had executed a fly that was so lifelike that when Cimabue returned to carry on with his work he tried several times to brush it off with his hand, under the impression that it was real, before he realized his mistake.

In the end, Giotto would paint the frescoes that restored three-dimensionality to western art. Since the fall of Rome, the iconish figures with gold-leafed halos adorning churches from Byzantium westward had looked more like cartoons than like life. After Giotto, they looked solid again. Vasari explains:

> Thus the old Byzantine style was completely abandoned—the first steps being taken by Cimabue and followed by Giotto—and a new style took its place: I like to call this Giotto's own style, since it was discovered by him and his pupils and was then generally admired and imitated by everybody. In this style of painting the unbroken outline was rejected, as well as staring eyes, feet on tiptoe, sharp hands, absence of shadow, and other Byzantine absurdities; these gave way to graceful heads and delicate colouring. Giotto, especially, posed his figures more attractively, started to show some animation in the heads, and by depicting his draperies in folds made them more realistic; his innovations to some extent included the art of foreshortening. As well as this, he was the first to express the emotions, so that in his pictures one can discern expressions of fear, hate, anger or love.

In other words, Giotto created the foundation for all Western art after the Middle Ages.

Vasari's life of Filippo Brunelleschi is also a revelation. As Giotto restored art to life, following the dark centuries, Brunelleschi revived the art of architecture. Vasari explains that:

> For hundreds of years men had neglected this art and had squandered their wealth on buildings without order, badly executed and poorly designed, which were full of strange inventions, shamefully devoid of grace and execrably ornamented.

It would be Brunelleschi who changed all that. Having lost an important commission to Lorenzo Ghiberti, Filippo set out with his pal Donatello to Rome, where they studied architecture and sculpture. Arriving in Rome, they were amazed: the grandeur and perfection of the ancient buildings were unlike anything Filippo and Donatello had expected. Filippo kept "stopping short in amazement, as if thunder-struck." Working together, Brunelleschi and Donatello began measuring the buildings, sketching them, drawing floor plans and elevations, and making careful studies of the details of their construction. Brunelleschi became obsessed:

> As Filippo had no domestic ties he was able to give himself completely to his studies, not caring whether he went without food and sleep and concentrating utterly on the architecture of the past...

He measured and sketched everything: all kinds of buildings, arches, cornices, columns, and techniques for binding stone to stone. He physically unearthed the remains of buildings and studied their features. And in the end, he returned to Florence, where he learned that the Florentines were preparing to put a great dome over the octagonal walls of their cathedral. The only problem was, no one knew how to do it. See, the octagonal building was big; the stone dome would have to span a space 139 feet across on top of walls 180 feet high! Seeing his chance, Fillipo returned to Rome; he "thought that he would be valued more highly if he had to be sought after than if he stayed in Florence."

The world knows that eventually Brunelleschi submitted his design, and eventually it was accepted. But the story of its acceptance is revealing. The tribunal that would appoint the dome architect asked all candidates to explain their ideas in detail, and Filippo refused. Instead, he suggested that:

> ...whoever could make an egg stand on end on a flat piece of marble should build the cupola, since this would show how intelligent each man was. So an egg was procured and the artists in turn tried to make it stand on end; but they were all unsuccessful. Then Filippo was asked to do so, and taking the egg graciously he cracked its bottom on the marble and made it stay upright. The others complained that they could have done as much, and laughing at them Filippo retorted that they would also have known how to vault the cupola if they had seen his model or plans.

Filippo got the job.

And it's a good dome, too. A beautiful dome. Even now, five hundred years later, Filippo's dome still rises gracefully above Florence, a testament to his genius for preparation, incubation, illumination, and verification (vide Wallas, 1926, studies in creative behavior!). How did he accomplish the dome's construction? Without even using interior scaffolding! The construction of the huge dome moved from the top of the walls upward and inward, with the workers supported only by the self-supporting stonework they were building. Drop a brick, and it would fall 200 feet to the interior floor. And the dome was not a dome; it was some domes. In order to solve the problem of the tremendous weight of the dome, Brunelleschi developed a brilliant design: one dome inside another, connected to each other, resulting in a dome that was light because it was hollow! Strong, too. Go see it. Fly to New York and take a right, cross the water, and land on the boot below the Alps.

Of course, the tribunal could not leave brilliant enough alone. They appointed Brunelleschi's old rival, Ghiberti, as a co-architect on the project, leaving Brunelleschi so mad he was spitting bricks. It was too much, especially since this dome was, so to speak, over Ghiberti's head. But Brunelleschi knew what to do:

> One morning or other Filippo failed to put in an appearance on the site; instead, he bandaged his head and took to his bed, and then, groaning all the time, he had everyone anxiously warming plates and cloths while he pretended to be suffering from colic. When they heard what was happening the master-builders who were standing around waiting for their instructions asked Lorenzo [Ghiberti] what they should do next. He replied that the schedule was Filippo's and that they would have to wait for him. One of the builders asked:
>
> "But don't you know what he has in mind?"

"Yes," said Lorenzo, "but I would do nothing without him."

Days passed. Work stopped. When the frustrated builders would ask the sick Filippo what they should do, he would reply, "You have Lorenzo; let him do something." Finally, they begged Filippo to return, but he said, "Oh, isn't that fellow Lorenzo there? Can he do nothing? I'm astonished—and at you too!" They answered, "He will do nothing without you." And then Filippo made his point: "I would do it well enough without him."

Perhaps sunlight broke through the clouds at those words. Perhaps not. But Ghiberti was shuffled aside to a hollow title and an undeserved salary, and Filippo Brunelleschi returned to the job, giving European civilization one of its loveliest accomplishments.

These stories about Giotto and Brunelleschi show the fascination of reading Vasari; more than any coffee table art book could do, Vasari takes you behind the scenes of the Renaissance and shows you the, the...well, the *lives of the artists*. In chapter after chapter, we read about the paintings and the sculptures, but we also read about the disputes, the jokes, the friendships, and the defiance of artists who, whether they realized it or not, were redefining the relationship between artist and society. I will not spoil the book by telling you any more of these stories...

Okay, one more.

When Leonardo da Vinci was young, he would walk past places where caged birds were sold, and he would buy birds, take them out of their cages, and release them into the air.

Freedom.

Now, that's all. No, read the book.

Aside from these stories of artists lives, there are other important merits to Vasari's famous work. One is the almost physical sense one feels about time, about history. Vasari keeps referring to his modern times, to modern artists, to the things modern artists have learned from studying ancient works. His talk feels so contemporary, so hip, so 20th century, so modern. Reading his sentences, we have to keep shaking off the cognitive dissonance we feel, because by modern, Vasari means 1550. He means modern artists like Leonardo, Raphael, and Michelangelo. You know, his modern contemporaries. How, we wonder, could he feel modern? He did not have electricity, or internal combustion engines, or computers, or Internets.

No, but he had something better: a new mental world. A new openness of thought. He had the Renaissance as his environment. He had Gutenberg's invention (a century earlier) to help with his book. He had the discovery of a new continent on the other side of the world to make things seem futuristic. He had the dark ages behind him, and shockingly original artists down every road, and popes supporting creative ideas with loads of cash. It was very modern. Why, Shakespeare and Cervantes were just around the corner. Even the United States was only two centuries in the future.

In the year 2550, what will our twenty-two-greats grandchildren think of our modern books, our modern society, and our modern ideas? They may feel more kinship with Vasari than they do with us, just as we often feel more kinship with Plato than we do with Robert E. Lee. (Do not get sore; if you are a Leeophile, then pick your own example.)

And so in addition to depicting the real lives of great

artists and explaining the artistic ideas of the Italian Renaissance, Vasari provides us with a time journey that awakens our sense of the reality of history.

It is a wondrous book, a book for which we would give anything if it did not exist and we were only imagining it. Imagine, what would we give to have a book by a guy who knew Michelangelo, who actually studied under him, who corresponded with him as an intimate friend?

But beyond all of these extraordinary qualities, Vasari's *Lives of the Artists* has another special aspect, something so unexpected and profound that at first one almost reads over it. Almost.

Vasari, we gradually realize with a chill that tickles our necks, was a distant survivor of ancient Armageddon. He was writing at a time when Europe was peeping out from its refuges, creeping out of its holes, digging out of its ruins. The Renaissance, we keep forgetting, was Mad Max Beyond Alaric the Visigoth. You remember Alaric. We're talking sculpture smashers. Guys with horns on their helmets. In chapter after chapter of Vasari's lives, we read about sculptures and buildings that had not yet been unearthed during the artist's lifetime. The ancient world was still buried. In fact, these are the first words of Vasari's book:

> The flood of misfortunes which continuously swept over and submerged the unhappy country of Italy not only destroyed everything worthy to be called a building but also, and this was of far greater consequence, completely wiped out the artists who lived there.

In his preface, Vasari explains that:

...almost all the barbarian nations rose up against the Romans in various parts of the world, and this within a short time led not only to the humbling of that great empire but also to worldwide destruction, notably at Rome itself. This destruction struck equally and decisively at the greatest artists, sculptors, painters, and architects: they and their work were left buried and submerged among the sorry ruins and debris of that renowned city.

Vasari then describes the destruction of the remaining pagan art by Christian zealots who wished to purge the world of every "occasion of sin" and who demolished statues, pictures, mosaics, and ornaments, as well as countless inscriptions and memorials of illustrious persons of the ancient world. But then:

As if these disasters were not enough, Rome then suffered the anger of Totila: the walls of the city were destroyed, its finest and most noble buildings were razed to the ground with fire and sword, and then it was burned from one end to the other, left bereft of every living creature and abandoned to the ravages of the conflagration.

Vasari says that Rome lost its identity and its very life. The ground floors of all the buildings were buried under the ruins. Eventually, those who survived planted vines on the rubble, and Rome was gone.

Gone.

In Vasari's modern day, five hundred years later, Italians were still digging out the debris of Rome's cataclysmic destruction, and Giotto was rediscovering painting; Brunelleschi was rediscovering architecture, and

Alberti was rediscovering perspective. Rediscovering.

Santyanna tells us that those who do not know history are condemned to repeat it.

Read Vasari.

TEN

The Day the Universe Changed

James Burke

Doubt increases with knowledge. - Goethe

One of the hurdles in learning to think philosophically is to reconsider the concept of knowledge. From our earliest years, we acquire a concept of knowledge from our social experience, and this concept leads us to understand that some things can be known; that is, their truth is completely and indubitably apprehended. When we know, the concept goes, we have gone above the mean strata of ignorance and doubt to a place of truth. Knowledge means reaching a point at which we can say that now we know. We have reached certainty. We now have knowledge.

What we know, we know.

We think.

Of course, every once in a while an anomaly shows us that some bit of knowledge was not really knowledge after all. Perhaps our perfectly clear and vivid memory of an event turns out to have been mistaken; we see in a video recording that what we are sure happened, did not, even though we experienced complete confidence in our recollection. Perhaps our direct observation of a social interaction makes us feel indignant that someone could be so intentionally rude, but we later learn that the mental states and intentions of those involved were not as we "saw" them at all, and our anger has been unjustly

72

directed at an innocent person. Perhaps we discover that a fact of history or science, as we thought we learned it, is wrong, or has been superseded by a more current "fact." Perhaps a new discovery renders an entire scientific theory outmoded, incomplete, or inaccurate; if that can happen to Newton, it can happen to anybody.

But...what is the difference between the knowledge that we know is knowledge and actually is knowledge, and the knowledge that we know is knowledge but actually is false and that we may or may not someday learn is false? How can we tell the bad "knowledge" from the good?

And...if we cannot tell the bad knowledge from the good knowledge now, at the time we think both are true, then is not all knowledge doubtful? And if knowledge is doubtful, then what is the difference between knowledge and doubt?

Socrates said, "I only know that I know nothing."

And we begin to see why.

Philosophers, of course, have struggled with these problems. After all, they are searching for truth, and if there can be no real knowledge, then . . .

The branch of philosophy that studies the problem of knowledge, its presuppositions and foundations, and its extent and validity is epistemology. Descartes was doing epistemology when he set out to prove the existence of God. Reasoning that reasoning based on falsehood could not be trusted, Descartes decided to begin with a proposition that was absolutely true and indisputable. And so he began searching for such an indisputable truth by a process of methodical doubting; anything he could doubt, he would cast aside.

The problem was, Descartes discovered that he could

doubt almost anything. Finding that his memory could be doubted, that his senses could be doubted, that his assumptions about reality could be doubted, he finally came up with something he could not doubt: that he was doubting. He could not doubt that he was doubting.

Bedrock.

The way he put it was, *Cogito, ergo sum*. I think, therefore I am.

Beginning with this *a priori* certainty, Descartes reasoned his way deductively to the existence of God.

Nice try. Of course, keen wits soon opined that Descartes had employed circular reasoning, begging the question by already assuming his conclusion, *I am*, in his premise, *I think*, for how could it be he thinking unless it was he thinking?

Knowing stuff, really knowing stuff, is more complicated than it seems on the surface. The surface, see, that is the problem. Because below the surface of knowledge are...well, assumptions. We assume that our eyes see right, and our ears hear right, and our interpretation interprets right, that we are awake, that we are sane, that the books we read for background were right, and the experts who provided our truths were right, and what we have been told is right, and our civilization's version of everything is right, and our culture's assumptions are right, and our questions are the right questions, and our words are the right words for the right things, and that we are...right. And if all the right stuff is right, then the knowledge is right.

Probably.

But what if these assumptions are wrong?

What if some of our most important basic ideas are just that—ideas?

What if our fundamental assumptions about this big thing we are in, the universe, suddenly turn out to be mistaken, and we have to change what we think?

That would be the day our view of the universe changed.

James Burke called his extraordinary book and video series *The Day the Universe Changed* for that reason; his focus is sharply on moments in intellectual history when a sudden discovery forced humanity to rethink a basic concept of reality.

What sudden discoveries?

Burke begins with the humanist self-confidence based on belief in reason. After St. Augustine's *City of God*, Europeans had seen a static, unchanging universe, created and maintained by God. Man's role in the universe was to live through unquestioning faith. With the rediscovery of Aristotle, thinkers like Peter Abelard began to view things differently. Abelard advocated not faith, but doubt, egad, as a path to truth. "By doubting we come to enquiry," Abelard said, "And by enquiring we perceive the truth." Using doubt and logic as powerful new instruments of the mind, Abelard, Bacon, and others turned understanding through belief into belief through understanding, and humanity's perception of its role in the universe was flipped.

Another day the universe changed was the day in the early 1400s when Brunelleschi—who later solved the dome design problem for the Florence cathedral—used a mirror trick that Toscanelli had shown him to produce the first Renaissance example of perspective painting. Burke explains that:

What had been achieved was a revolution in the way

people looked at the world, not just in terms of visual representation but from a philosophical point of view. Following the discovery of perspective geometry, the position of man in the cosmos altered. The new technique permitted the world to be measured through proportional comparison.

Suddenly, instead of seeing themselves in terms of their theological sizes, human beings began to view themselves in terms that had nothing to do with religion. Perspective geometry permitted a new, objective, mathematically based understanding of the universe in which humanity had its own measurable proportion.

And perspective geometry was just the beginning. Next up was the fact. The fact that what? Just the fact, ma'am. See, before the invention of the printing press, learning could not be widely disseminated, especially not in a uniform presentation, because every book had to be tediously hand-copied. The monks were in the middle. After Gutenberg, *Johannes Gansfleisch zur Laden zum Gutenberg*, to be precise, there could be books. For everybody. Mass-produced books. And suddenly, claims could be studied, and examined, and checked for accuracy. Once civilization had the mass-produced books that allowed widespread checking of details, it suddenly had details that checked out; it had facts. Burke says that "Printing was to bring about the most radical alteration ever made in Western intellectual history." Why? Because now knowledge could be had from a book, and both the oral society and the age of unquestioned authority were over. Now, every thinking individual who was literate could check things for himself or herself. It was dazzling. Burke says, "The presses opened the way to all who could read to share for the first time in the world's collective knowledge, to explore the minds of others, and to approach the mysteries of nature with confidence instead of awe."

For example? Well that brings up another day the universe changed. One of the newfangled printed books was by a man named Koppernigk. We call him Copernicus, and his book *On the Revolution of the Celestial Spheres* was revolutionary. The way he saw it, Aristotle's traditional geocentric view of the cosmos, with humanity's earth at the center and everything going reverently round it, was for the birds. As a matter of fact, he concluded, the sun was the center of a heliocentric solar system, and the earth and all of the other planets were only the sun's measly satellites. It was we who were in humble revolution. And this was too revolutionary for the church, which said that according to the holy writ of Aristotle (huh?), geocentrism was the Truth. Koppernigk blamed heliocentrism on Pythagoras and Aristarchus and kept his profile low. But the revolutions were out of the bag, and soon Galileo found moons around Jupiter, and Desartes said it was time to start doubting everything— remember?

In the 1700s the social universe changed. John Locke had prepared the philosophical ground for social revolution in the previous century in his *Two Treatises on Government*. Locke argued that people are driven by self-interest, that governments should let them pursue it, and that the relationship between government and its citizens is a sort of contract. Locke argued that legislative and executive power should be separate to avoid tyranny,and that the ultimate goal of government is to preserve the property rights of the individual.

But this was before technology made the explosive growth of industry possible. In Locke's time, manufacturing was still labor-intensive, and slavery was the way to get big things done. Enter the Scottish instrument-maker who changed the universe of work, James Watt. His breakthrough in creating an efficient steam engine gave steam to the industrial revolution, to a degree that is still astonishing:

> Some years after the beginning of the nineteenth century it was noted that a factory using one 100 hp steam engine did the work equal to 880 men. It ran 50,000 spindles, employed 750 workers and produced 226 times more than it had done before the introduction of steam....
>
> The Industrial Revolution also gave birth to socialism, and the social separation of society through the division of labor. It brought science and industry together in a new and dynamic relationship. It radically altered the shape of the country and the behaviour of its citizens. And it made modern urban society dependent on mass-production techniques without which we cannot now survive.

And then in the 1800s there was the medical revolution. In the space of a few decades, scientists and doctors developed anesthetics, vaccinations, and medical statistics. They discovered the causes of plague, cholera, gonorrhea, streptococcus, diphtheria, typhoid, tetanus, and syphilis. The formerly important role of the patient in explaining his own diagnosis vanished, leaving the doctor as the authoritative expert. One led to another:

> By the beginning of the twentieth century the techniques developed by the medical profession over the previous hundred years were being adopted in a

wider social context. The change in the condition of the body physical, with its new subjection to more impersonal treatment, its removal from the role of decision-maker to that of passive patient, its reduction to number and statistical analysis, the establishment of "laws" against which the patient is powerless and insufficiently informed to argue, has been mirrored in the condition of the body social. As individualism gives way to regulation by number, society is well on the way to being cured for its own good, whether it likes it or not.

In all of Burke's changes, the individual's sense of who and what he or she is goes through a dramatic shift, but none of them, perhaps, requires the complete reassessment of reality that has occurred in the wake of modern physics, with its overthrow of Newton. You remember Newton, the preeminent scientific genius who gave us a stable, mathematical, homey cosmos, with universal time, universal space, and calculus to measure it all. Enter the Wild Bunch, of scientists, that is: Rogues and ne'er-do-wells, like Faraday, Maxwell, Michelson, Mach, Einstein, Planck, and Heisenberg. By the time they were done with the universe, Newton's universals and constants were in shambles, the continuum of energy had been crumbled into quanta, absolute time had melted into relativity, and Heisenberg had looked demon uncertainty straight in the eye:

In 1927 Heisenberg showed that it could never be determined which phenomenon [light waves or light particles] was occurring, as both were products of the instruments. Either an experiment could look for particles and find them, or it could look for waves and find them too, but not both at once.

He also noted that particles could never be observed with certainty. Either their momentum could be studied through observation of the wave form in which they travelled, or their position could be established by stopping them in flight. Each examination precluded the other. We could say where an electron was or how fast it was going, but not both. Moreover, the act of observation itself would complicate matters. In order to "see" the electron it would be necessary to shine a light of some kind on it. This would add to the energy of the electron and alter its state or position. In the act of observation the universe was changed. As Heisenberg said, in a statement that finally ended the speculation begun in the eighteenth century, "If we want to describe what happens in an atomic event, we have to realise that the word "happens" can apply only to the observation, not the state of affairs between the two observations."

The investigation of electricity led to an entirely new view of the universe and of the ability of science to say anything about it. It destroyed the cause-and-effect view that had ruled since the time of Thales, in ancient Greece.

If, as Heisenberg suggested, every description of reality contains some essential and irretrievable uncertainty and the observer, in observing, modifies the phenomenon, then, as Wittgenstein said, "You see what you want to see." The universe is what we say it is. However, if this is so, what is knowledge?

In his final chapter, "Worlds Without End," Burke assesses the significance of these changing universes. He finds that science is not what it appears to be, objective and impartial, because every scientific observation is impregnated with theory. And theory, he notes, dictates what the "facts" shall be, which in turn "prove" the theory. The argument of science, Burke therefore says, is circular. The implications of this are that "since the structure of reality changes over time, science can only answer contemporary questions about a reality defined in contemporary terms and investigated with contemporary tools."

Knowledge, Burke concludes, is man-made. "The universe is what we say it is. When theories change the universe changes. The truth is relative."

Interestingly, in the video version only, Burke follows this point with a powerful corollary: If the universe is what we say it is, then say.

Yes, perhaps knowledge is not what we thought. Perhaps we can not really know our knowledge, and the "real" universe will always be hidden beyond our theories and veiled by our assumptions. If so, as Burke realizes, it is all the more reason to live with high intent.

ELEVEN

Shakespearean Tragedy

A.C. Bradley

There is a certain joy that accompanies the discovery of a loved one feared lost. He's alive, we cry, and sink into a swimming happiness.

So it is for lovers of A.C. Bradley's *Shakespearean Tragedy*. He's alive, in a third edition, and all of us who mourned his disappearance and who cursed the difficulty of finding fading copies of his classic literary analysis in moldy used book bins can now breathe again.

Do not laugh, either.

Andrew Bradley (1851-1935) was Professor of Poetry at the University of Oxford, and his classic collection of ten lectures on *Hamlet*, *Othello*, *King Lear*, and *Macbeth* represents, for many readers, the most lucid and penetrating, the most human—the most cherished—analysis of Shakespeare's tragedies. Called simply *Shakespearean Tragedy*, Bradley's masterpiece was first published in the U.K. in 1904, first published in the United States in 1957, and was then reprinted in 1957, 1959, 1961, 1962, 1963, and 1964. And then?

And then, impossibly, the thing vanished. Lord, what fools we mortals be. I well remember the distress I felt ten years ago, when I blithely assumed that it would be easy to get a new copy of a book so beautiful, only to be telephonically repulsed by the big book chains, who had never heard of it. In an egad sweat, I drove across Durham, North Carolina, to find and scour an immense used book store, and after inhaling more than my fair share of dust mites, I unearthed a dog-eared, broken-backed copy of *Shakespearean Tragedy* to replace the beloved copy I had given to a friend.

Whew.

That was close.

Shakespearean Tragedy is a book that one cannot be without.

Why?

Well, that takes some explaining.

In *Shakespearean Tragedy*, we have, preserved through the miracle of print, A.C. Bradley's famous lectures to the students of Oxford. These are not, in our sense, essays. They are lectures; they are the elaborate, eloquent, and elegant transcripts of Bradley's lectures to his scholars. Imagine it: turn-of-the-century Oxford, the wood-paneled walls, the unairconditioned classroom, the great scholar, the students, the eye contact. Imagine that you could have Oxford's most famous Shakespeare professor as your own teacher; with this book, you can. And like Kenneth Clark, Bradley is articulate and courteous and uses the English language with a patience and refinement that is scarcely available in any book written today.

And then, there are the ideas.

Reading Bradley is like having a CAT scan for plays. He works comfortably at a depth far into the play, where every character is alive, and every word blooms out into a reality.

Bradley begins with two preliminary lectures—one on the substance of Shakespearean tragedy, and one on construction in Shakespeare's tragedies. This is followed by two lectures on *Hamlet*, two on *Othello*, two on *King Lear*, and two on *Macbeth*.

In the first lecture, "The Substance of Shakespearean Tragedy," Bradley considers the problem of tragedy, that central tragic condition that the tragedies as a group have in common. About tragedy as it appears in Shakespeare's plays, Bradley makes a number of observations: that there are a considerable number of persons in the plays; that the tragedy is concerned primarily with one person; that it leads to that person's death; that the suffering and calamity are exceptional and unexpected; that they extend far and wide beyond the central figure, making the whole scene a scene of woe; that the tragedies befall persons of high degree; that they proceed from the actions of men; that the actions issue from character; that there are abnormal conditions of mind, but that these abnormal conditions are never the origin of tragic deeds; that there are supernatural elements such as ghosts and witches, but that these elements are also not the cause of the tragedy; that there is a significant presence of chance in the plays, but that chance is not responsible for the tragic events; that the tragedies demonstrate a conflict of forces in the hero's soul.

Good, you think. But Bradley is only warming up. Still in the first lecture, he turns his attention to the nature of the central figure, and he observes that the central figures of Shakespeare's tragedies are exceptional beings, that in real life we have known scarcely anyone resembling them, that...wait, let me quote Bradley here; he says that Shakespeare's:

> ...tragic characters are made of the stuff we find within ourselves and within the persons who surround them. But, by an intensification of the life which they share with others, they are raised above them; and the greatest are raised so far that, if we fully realize all

that is implied in their words and actions, we become conscious that in real life we have known scarcely any one resembling them. Some, like Hamlet and Cleopatra, have genius. Others, like Othello, Lear, Macbeth, Coriolanus, are built on the grand scale; and desire, passion, or will attains in them a terrible force. In almost all we observe a marked one-sidedness, a predisposition in some particular direction; a total incapacity, in certain circumstances, of resisting the force which draws in this direction; a fatal tendency to identify the whole being with one interest, object, passion, or habit of mind. This, it would seem, is, for Shakespeare, the fundamental tragic trait.

And then Bradley sharpens the point: "In the circumstances where we see the hero placed, his tragic trait, which is also his greatness, is fatal to him." This painful irony leads Bradley to the recognition of waste:

And with this greatness of the tragic hero...is connected, secondly, what I venture to describe as the centre of the tragic impression. This central feeling is the impression of waste. With Shakespeare, at any rate, the pity and fear which are stirred by the tragic story seem to unite with, and even to merge in, a profound sense of sadness and mystery, which is due to this impression of waste. "What a piece of work is man," we cry; "so much more beautiful and so much more terrible than we knew! Why should he be so if this beauty and greatness only tortures itself and throws itself away?" We seem to have before us a type of the mystery of the whole world, the tragic fact which extends far beyond the limits of tragedy.

And Bradley brings this thought to its highest point: that tragedy "forces the mystery upon us, and makes us realize so vividly the worth of that which is wasted that we cannot possibly seek comfort in the reflection that all is vanity." Here, incomparably put, is the reply to all of us who view tragedy as essentially negative.

But notice Bradley's Socratic tolerance of the unknown, of the wild and dark universe that shimmers and quakes somewhere beyond human comprehension. For Bradley, the known and the unknown are mysteriously unified but cognitively differentiated. His thinking is more than ordinary literary analysis:

> We remain confronted with the inexplicable fact, or the no less inexplicable appearance, of a world travailing for perfection, but bringing to birth, together with glorious good, an evil which it is able to overcome only by self-torture and self-waste. And this fact or appearance is tragedy.

The second lecture, on the construction of Shakespeare's tragedies, is perhaps less profound but nonetheless technically interesting to anyone smitten with Shakespearean tragedy. Bradley divides the plays into the exposition, the development of the conflict, and the catastrophe. The purpose of the exposition, he says prettily, is to "introduce us into a little world of persons." The development involves a "constant alternation of rises and falls in [the] tension or in the emotional pitch of the work, a regular sequence of more exciting and less exciting sections." These developments lead to a critical point, a turning point, a crisis, after which the hero plunges into catastrophe and death.

Bradley examines these structures in elaborate

detail, giving numerous examples and (characteristic of his integrity) exceptions. But in discussing the fine points of construction, Bradley turns his attention to a question that has plagued many a literary conversation: To what extent does the author, in this case Shakespeare, use artistic devices consciously? Is the author working as a deliberate artist, employing the elements of drama and poetry for intentional effect, or is the artist drifting in inspiration, moving in the moment of the muse, unaware of the technical elements of construction and poetry that happen fortuitously as a product of the gift? In other words, did Shakespeare think to himself, Now I will construct an exposition, followed by alternating degrees of intense development? Did Shakespeare think to himself, For this scene I will use regular meter and end-rhyme to emphasize the nobility of my character? Bradley's answer may surprise you; some of his readers, he says:

> ...may have asked themselves whether I have not used the words "art" and "device" and "expedient" and "method" too boldly, as though Shakespeare were a conscious artist, and not rather a writer who constructed in obedience to an extraordinary dramatic instinct, as he composed mainly by inspiration....In speaking, for convenience, of devices and expedients, I did not intend to imply that Shakespeare always deliberately aimed at the effects which he produced. But no artist always does this, and I see no reason to doubt that Shakespeare often did it, or to suppose that his method of constructing and composing differed, except in degree, from that of the most "conscious" of artists. The antithesis of art and inspiration, though not meaningless, is often most misleading.

Inspiration is surely not incompatible with considerate workmanship. The two may be severed, but they need not be so, and where a genuinely poetic result is being produced they cannot be so.

For the obdurate and intransigent skeptic who cannot believe that Shakespeare was a lowly "conscious" artist, Bradley adds that we know Shakespeare revised and rewrote such works as *Love's Labour's Lost, Romeo and Juliet,* and *Hamlet.* Bradley asks what ground we have for doubting that Shakespeare used art less consciously than other good poets. And finally Bradley brings the full force of reason against the idea that Shakespeare could not have been a conscious artist:

> But perhaps the notion of a "conscious artist" in drama is that of one who studies the theory of the art, and even writes with an eye to its "rules." And we know it was long a favourite idea that Shakespeare was totally ignorant of the "rules." Yet this is quite incredible. The rules referred to, such as they were, were not buried in Aristotle's Greek nor even hidden away in Italian treatises. He could find pretty well all of them in a book so current and famous as Sidney's *Defense of Poetry.* Even if we suppose that he refused to open this book (which is most unlikely) how could he possibly remain ignorant of the rules in a society of actors and dramatists and amateurs who must have been incessantly talking about plays and playwriting, and some of whom were ardent champions of the rules and full of contempt for the lawlessness of the popular drama?

Resistance crumbles. And before the reader can catch

his breath, or her breath, as gender may be, Bradley uses his triumph to turn the idea: If Shakespeare knew the so-called rules, then why did he often ignore them? And down we plunge, chasing with Bradley after the fleeting mind of a creative genius.

If Bradley's book ended here, having discussed the nature of tragedy and the construction of tragedies, it would be a landmark in literary criticism. But now he turns to the plays, and the real shooting starts.

That's the good news. The bad news is, I am not going to review the six lectures devoted to the plays because that would spoil the fun, or the thunder, if not the broth. Instead, I want to focus on Bradley's two lectures on *Hamlet* to see, not so much what he says, but how he says it.

Wait.

Do not put this book down.

Why? you ask.

Because it is here, in the lectures on *Hamlet*, that Bradley provides modern readers, teachers, and students with a model of literary reasoning.

For all of us who have felt unable to write about literature adequately, for all of us who have not really known how to make a case about an interpretation, for all of us who needed an explanation of techniques that would help us explicate a text, Bradley offers a model.

Of course, Bradley does reach important conclusions about *Hamlet* and Hamlet. He notes that in the play, Hamlet is the only figure of tragic proportions and that, "in Hamlet's absence, the remaining characters could not yield a Shakespearean tragedy at all." He finds that the character of Hamlet has exerted a greater fascination and has been the subject of more discussion "than any other in the whole literature of the world." He sees that Hamlet's character—specifically, the reason for his delay in sweeping to his revenge—is the central question of the play. He finds in Hamlet not only an "exquisite sensibility" but intellectual genius:

> Hamlet's intellectual power is not a specific gift, like a genius for music or mathematics or philosophy. It shows itself, fitfully, in the affairs of life as unusual quickness of perception, great agility in shifting the mental attitude, a striking rapidity and fertility in resource; so that, when his natural belief in others does not make him unwary, Hamlet easily sees through them and masters them, and no one can be much less like the typical helpless dreamer.

In exploring Hamlet's character, Bradley discovers that this combination of exquisite sensibility and intellectual genius—Hamlet's great strength—is the very weakness that brings him to tragedy because it leaves him fatally vulnerable to his own best qualities. Bradley observes that:

> ...under conditions of a peculiar kind, [the death of his father and the o'er hasty marriage of his mother] Hamlet's reflectiveness might prove dangerous to him, and his genius might even (to exaggerate a little) become his doom. Suppose that violent shock to his moral being of which I spoke; and suppose that under this shock, any possible action being denied to him, he began to sink into melancholy; then, no doubt, his imaginative and generalizing habit of mind might extend the effects of this shock through his whole being and mental world.

A less sensitive or less intelligent soul would have avoided paralysis, melancholy, and the reverberation of shock "through his whole being and mental world." But Hamlet is a tragic figure whose exceptional spirit fastens his doom upon him. With a kind of tenderness, Bradley concludes his third lecture:

> It was not that *Hamlet* is Shakespeare's greatest tragedy or most perfect work of art; it was that *Hamlet* most brings home to us at once the sense of the soul's infinity, and the sense of the doom which not only circumscribes that infinity but appears to be its offspring.

It is a fine thing to stand in the glow of Bradley's analysis, viewing the clarified play-things and feeling somehow illuminated oneself. But it is especially instructive to step back from Bradley's page, and look not at his conclusions, but at his methods, for in his literary reasoning Bradley uses a nice set of tools that we may profitably borrow.

For instance?

For instance, Socratic humility. As penetrating as his analysis is, it is not final, even to Bradley himself. At the beginning of the fourth lecture, he says:

> The only way, if there is any way, in which a conception of Hamlet's character could be proved true, would be to show that it, and it alone, explains all the relevant facts presented by the text of the drama. To attempt such a demonstration here would obviously be impossible, even if I felt certain of the interpretation of all the facts.

Such a healthy and authentic awareness of the difficulty of interpretation and of the limitations of one's own perceptions is an essential force in keeping the mind open and the questions alive.

A second characteristic of Bradley's reasoning is, to borrow Coleridge's phrase, a suspension of disbelief. For Bradley, Hamlet is not a phantom of words, a mere character; he is real. Bradley does not disbelieve the play just because he knows intellectually that it is an artwork of fiction. Rather, he imaginatively enters into the world of the play, which draws its reality from the genius of the playwright. Marianne Moore defined poems as imaginary gardens with real toads in them. For Bradley, Hamlet is a real toad. Bradley knows Hamlet as a person, analyzes his psychology, studies his feelings and reactions. Listen to Bradley, here discussing Hamlet's melancholy:

"Melancholy," I said, not dejection, nor yet insanity. That Hamlet was not far from insanity is very probable. His adoption of the pretence of madness may well have been due in part to fear of the reality; to an instinct of self-preservation, a fore-feeling that the pretence would enable him to give some utterance to the load that pressed on his heart and brain, and a fear that he would be unable altogether to repress such utterance.

Or here, describing the fateful timing that destroys Hamlet:

And this is the time which his fate chooses. In this hour of uttermost weakness, this sinking of his whole being towards annihilation, there comes on him, bursting the bounds of the natural world with a shock of astonishment and terror, the revelation of his mother's adultery and his father's murder, and, with this, the demand on him, in the name of everything dearest and most sacred, to arise and act.

Bradley also manifests a genuine belief in meaning. For A.C. Bradley, a Shakespearean tragedy does not mean "whatever it means to you." Rather, the play is a thing-in-itself, a little world of persons rotating around a central doomed figure, and in this little world, there is a central question. It is the question of the little world, not the question of the reader. The modern world's black void of naive relativism is not present in the cosmos of Bradley's literary reasoning. Although Bradley does not claim final understanding or deny that various intelligent things could be predicated about the play, he nonetheless waves the banner of its meaning, as here, where he dismisses a variety of views as lunatic:

> And we will confine our attention to sane theories; —for on this subject, as on all questions relating to Shakespeare, there are plenty of merely lunatic views: the view, for example, that Hamlet, being a disguised woman in love with Horatio, could hardly help seeming unkind to Ophelia; or the view that, being a very clever and wicked young man who wanted to oust his innocent uncle from the throne, he "faked" the ghost with this intent.

Hooray. And Bradley does not stop there. Gathering steam, he adds that "no theory will hold water which finds the cause of Hamlet's delay merely, or mainly, or even to any considerable extent, in external difficulties." Not even, we note, if that is what it means to you.

For those who doubt that Bradley can back those strong words up with sufficient force, he has an overwhelming weapon, the authority of the text. Describing the theory that Hamlet's difficulties are primarily external, rather than internal, Bradley states: "A theory like this sounds very plausible—so long as you do not remember the text." In the Oxford classroom, Bradley's eyes must have sparkled with the intent of this sentence, aimed at the base villain, falsehood. Imagine the opposition collapsing in panic as Bradley continued:

> A theory like this sounds very plausible—so long as you do not remember the text. But no unsophisticated mind, fresh from the reading of *Hamlet* will accept it; and, as soon as we begin to probe it, fatal objections will arise in such numbers that I choose but a few, and indeed I think the first of them is enough.

And then, Bradley delivers. A torrent of references to the text and quotations from the text pours forth, washing away all objections. Hamlet's difficulties are external? Then why does Hamlet never make the slightest reference to any external difficulty? Why does Hamlet always assume that he can obey the Ghost? Why does Hamlet say to himself that he has cause and will and strength and means to do it? Why does Hamlet plan the play-scene to convince himself that the Ghost had spoken the truth? Why does Hamlet never talk of bringing the King to public justice, but rather always speaks of using his sword or his arm? Fatal objections, indeed.

Bradley next turns on the idea that Hamlet is simply restrained by conscience from killing his uncle. Again, Bradley raises the sword of text:

This idea, like the first, can easily be made to look very plausible, if we vaguely imagine the circumstances without attending to the text. But attention to the text is fatal to it.

And it is not just that Bradley produces the text as a refutation of all nonsense; it is the way he does it. One of his most powerful techniques for citing the text is the summary cluster. Refuting Goethe's sentimental view of Hamlet as a moral weakling "without the strength of nerve which forms a hero," Bradley draws an array of succinct descriptions from the entire play and demolishes the view:

> But consider the text. This shrinking, flower-like youth—how could he possibly have done what we see Hamlet do? What likeness to him is there in the Hamlet who, summoned by the Ghost, bursts from his terrified friends with the cry: "Unhand me, gentlemen! By heaven, I'll make a ghost of him that lets me"; the Hamlet who scarcely once speaks to the King without an insult, or to Polonius without a gibe; the Hamlet who storms at Ophelia and speaks daggers to his mother; the Hamlet who, hearing a cry behind the arras, whips out his sword in an instant and runs the eavesdropper through; the Hamlet who sends his "school-fellows" to their death and never troubles his head about them more; the Hamlet who is the first man to board a pirate ship, and who fights with Laertes in the grave; the Hamlet of the catastrophe, an omnipotent fate, before whom all the court stands helpless, who, as the truth breaks upon him, rushes on the King, drives his foil right through his body, then seizes the poisoned cup and forces it violently

between the wretched man's lips, and in the throes of death has force and fire enough to wrest the cup from Horatio's hand ("By heaven, I'll have it!") lest he should drink and die? This man, the Hamlet of the play, is a heroic, terrible figure. He would have been formidable to Othello or Macbeth. If the sentimental Hamlet had crossed him, he would have hurled him from his path with one sweep of his arm.

Bradley condenses nine refutations into one paragraph, creating a preponderance of evidence that overwhelms intellectual resistance. In this paragraph, Bradley is not quoting or even paraphrasing. He is constructing a tight series of concrete summaries or references to the text—reminders—that allow the reader to consider an idea in light of the facts of the play. When Bradley describes "the Hamlet who scarcely once speaks to the King without an insult," this is not a quote or even a paraphrase, but we recognize it at once as an accurate summary of numerous lines in the play where Hamlet's responses to Claudius are cold and ironic.

Sometimes Bradley swiftly incorporates short quotes and paraphrases into a summary cluster, as here, where he attacks the idea that Hamlet couldn't sweep to his revenge because he was one-sidedly reflective:

> ...the text does not bear out the idea that he was one-sidedly reflective and indisposed to action. Nobody who knew him seems to have noticed this weakness. Nobody regards him as a mere scholar who has "never formed a resolution or executed a deed." In a court which certainly would not much admire such a person he is the observed of all observers. Though he has been disappointed of the throne everyone shows

him respect; and he is the favourite of the people, who are not given to worship philosophers. Fortinbras, a sufficiently practical man, considered that he was likely, had he been put on, to have proved most royally. He has Hamlet borne by four captains "like a soldier" to his grave; and Ophelia says that he was a soldier. If he was fond of acting, an aesthetic pursuit, he was equally fond of fencing, an athletic one: he practiced it assiduously even in his worst days.

See how Bradley combines summaries, paraphrases, and snips of quotation (observed of all observers, proved most royally) in a way that grounds his argument solidly in the text.

The text: attention to the text is the center of quality literary reasoning. Again and again, Bradley reminds us of the importance of the text. "But consider the text," he says. "Attention to the text is fatal" to an idea, he says. A theory is plausible, he says, "so long as you do not remember the text."

Another technique that Bradley uses to build a case out of the text is the quote cluster, though Bradley often depends upon the reader's knowledge of the play and dispenses with quotation marks. Bradley deftly weaves a series of direct quotations from the text into a fabric of persuasion:

There were no old truths for Hamlet. It is for Horatio a thing of course that there's a divinity that shapes our ends, but for Hamlet it is a discovery hardly won. And throughout this kindom of the mind, where he felt that man, who in action is only like an angel, is in apprehension like a god, he moved (we must imagine) more than content, so that even in his dark days he declares he could be bounded in a nutshell and yet count himself a king of infinite space, were it not that he had bad dreams.

This is beautifully done. Bradley is using the language of the play, turning it back on itself, allowing the play to be a self-interpreting work of literary art. In Bradley's literary reasoning, the language of the play itself, the text, is the construction material. The work of art provides the interpreter with the terms for its own interpretation.

Bradley also uses word *focus* to make his point. In a quotation cluster, he will italicize the most germane words, lifting them to the reader's attention. In discussing Hamlet's apathy or lethargy, Bradley notes, "We are bound to consider the evidence which the text supplies of this, though it is usual to ignore it." He continues:

So, in the soliloquy in II. ii., he accuses himself of being "a dull and muddy-mettled rascal", who "peaks [mopes] like John-a-dreams, unpregnant of his cause", dully indifferent to his cause. So, when the Ghost appears to him the second time, he accuses himself of being tardy and lapsed in time; and the Ghost speaks of his purpose as being almost blunted, and bids him not to forget.

This technique creates, in essence, a series of one-word quotations, a body of text quanta that brings the case to its sharpest focus.

Bradley's masterful analysis of Shakespeare's tragedies, featuring Socratic humility, the suspension of disbelief, a belief in meaning, the authority of the text, summary clusters, the incorporation of short quotes (with or without quotation marks) and paraphrases, and italicized focus on words, is a model of superb literary reasoning. In reading Bradley we learn about Shakespeare's tragedies, but beyond that, we learn what the literary reasoning process—at its highest levels of quality and integrity—is like.

There are few works of literary criticism that are themselves as classic as the works they discuss. This is one of them.

TWELVE

Ellen Foster

Kaye Gibbons

I keep remembering Marianne Moore's haunting definition: poems are imaginary gardens with real toads in them.

Many of our gifted children—many of the ones we know, understand, and love best—are characters in fiction. But to call them fictional characters is misleading because it implies that they are not real.

Well, *au contraire.*

Fiction may be imaginary, but it is an imaginary path to reality. Through fiction we can dig to the truth of the truth, can transcend the ordinary confines of self, and can visit the souls of our others.

A.C. Bradley called *Hamlet* "a little world of persons." And that is what it is. A little world. With persons.

If you want to fight about it, tell me that my favorite gifted characters are not real.

Go ahead; make my day.

Consider some of literature's most gifted characters. There is, for example, Scout Finch, the Harper Lee girl, who gets in trouble at school because she could already read when she got there. It made the teacher mad—angry, actually—and she scolded Atticus, Scout's dad. In the end, Scout takes the reclusive Boo Radley home, holding his hand:

Boo and I walked up the steps to the porch. His fingers found the front doorknob. He gently released my hand, opened the door, went inside, and shut the door behind him. I never saw him again.

Neighbors bring food with death and flowers with sickness and little things in between. Boo was our neighbor. He gave us two soap dolls, a broken watch and chain, a pair of good-luck pennies, and our lives. But neighbors give in return. We never put back into the tree what we took out of it: we had given him nothing, and it made me sad.

I turned to go home. Street lights winked down the street all the way to town. I had never seen our neighborhood from this angle....Atticus was right. One time he said you never really know a man until you stand in his shoes and walk around in them. Just standing on the Radley porch was enough.

Wise words, these ethical reflections of a gifted girl. *To Kill a Mockingbird* gives us a precious gift: an imaginary southern town with a real little girl in it. And this is a little girl we are profoundly grateful to know.

We are also grateful to know Tom Sawyer, the imaginative dreamer who is a natural leader, who enrolls all the kids in every project, who ambuscades the A-rabs, and who gets his fence painted. His mind is a kind of Tom-in-wonderland, where every life scene is actually a creative romantic adventure.

And there is young Jim Hawkins (Mistah 'Awkins, is it?) who sets sail on the high seas, summons up his courage, yo-ho-hos, spars with the brilliant Long John Silver, and survives through sheer creative intelligence and quick thinking. A good lad, he. Or, a good lad, 'ee.

Romeo and Juliet are little more than children when

they meet, but their good hearts and brilliant minds make them an instant match for each other. Their first words to each other form a witty stichomythia, a playful repartee in which each magnetically recognizes the other's quickness. Leave it to Shakespeare to craft their young words into a sonnet built for two.

And there is Hawthorne's Pearl, and Golding's Piggy, and Carroll's Alice.

These characters have lived in the human mind for ages and have enriched the acquaintances of generations of readers.

But new children keep becoming new writers, who keep imagining new children, who keep becoming new characters made of printed sentences, who become real in new readers' minds.

A very few new characters appear with a vividness and a truth of personality that makes them instant individuals, members of our minds, like our moms, or our friends, or our Heathcliff.

Like Ellen Foster.

Ellen Foster is the main character of Kaye Gibbons's first novel, *Ellen Foster*. First published by Chapel Hill's Algonquin Books in 1987, *Ellen Foster* surprised the reading community with its command of character and language, its maturity (this is a first novel?), and its depth. It won the Sue Kaufman Prize of the American Academy and Institute of Arts and Letters, and received a special citation from the Ernest Hemingway Foundation.

Kaye Gibbons must have been ecstatic because she received accolades from the foremost writers of our time. Walker Percy called *Ellen Foster* breathtaking, heartwrenching. Eudora Welty praised the life and the honesty. Alfred Kazin said it had the wickedest relatives since *King Lear*. And Elizabeth Spencer said that "the voice of Ellen Foster makes the reader know her story in her own terms."

Well, we should say so. Gibbons's Ellen Foster is an eleven-year-old girl, the poor-white-treasure daughter of a poor-white-trash alcoholic father and his destroyed wife. The family environment has all that it takes to destroy the daughter, too, but Ellen Foster will not have that. She is a survivor, a defender of her territories, a self-anointer who proclaims her own worth as a person with a right to live.

She is very human, but she is tough. When her daddy passes out drunk in the bathroom, she takes command:

> By the time the dog races come on he's stretched out on the bathroom floor and can't get up. I know I need to go in there and poke him....
>
> I get up and go in there and tell him to get up that folks got to come in there and do their business. He can go lay in the truck.
>
> He just grunts and grabs at my ankle and misses.
>
> Get on up I say again to him. You got to be firm when he is like this. He'd lay there and rot if I let him so I nudge him with my foot. I will not touch my hands to him. Makes me want to heave my own self seeing him pull himself up on the sink. He zig-zags out through the living room and I guess he makes it out the door. I don't hear him fall down the steps.

Do you hear the voice? Kaye Gibbons has found the real voice of this child, and it speaks through her pen. The child's cliches. The thin vocabulary. The shifting address and parentheticals. The solecisms. But then there are the exact details of dog races and truck beds. There is the will to act: "You got to be firm when he is like this."

There is the perfect authenticity of southern diction: poke him, do their business, my own self, makes me want to heave. And there is the intense awareness that Ellen takes for granted, because it is the only awareness that she has ever known: "I don't hear him fall down the steps."

From the first moment of our acquaintance, we feel the fibre and truth of this girl. In fact, here is the first moment of our acquaintance:

> When I was little I would think of ways to kill my daddy. I would figure out this or that way and run it down through my head until it got easy.
>
> The way I liked best was letting go a poisonous spider in his bed. It would bite him and he'd be dead and swollen up and I would shudder to find him so....
>
> But I did not kill my daddy. He drank his own self to death the year after the County moved me out. I heard how they found him shut up in the house dead and everything. Next thing I know he's in the ground and the house is rented out to a family of four.

There, see? Not since *Moby Dick* has an American novel been so fully born in so few words. In the fourth sentence of *Moby Dick*, Melville's Ishmael describes the damp, drizzly November in his soul, admits to involuntarily pausing before coffin warehouses and bringing up the rear of every funeral he meets, and confesses to wanting to step into the street and methodically knock people's hats off. (We would pay a lot to see this.) Ishmael concludes that it is high time to get to sea as soon as he can.

The opening sentence of *Ellen Foster* is at least this profound. How much deeper in the soul can one be than the conscious desire for patricide? And yet, we are not confronted by a bad child, a murderous personality; we see the thinking, the creative imagination, the self-humor (I would shudder to find him so), the acknowledgment of justice (He drank his own self to death), and the terrible realism in one so young (he's in the ground and the house is rented out to a family of four).

We begin to care about Ellen right away. In three paragraphs, we know her, we want to protect her, and we realize that she intends to protect herself. She is, we sense, exactly what she calls herself: Old Ellen. She is old. She is only eleven, but she has seen and survived things that no one her age should even know about. Her home is dominated by an abusive, alcoholic father, bitter and blaming the world for his inadequacy. She is not overwhelmed by an overwhelming environment of vulgarity, ignorance, indifference, surrender, and despair. She has had to be the adult, to comfort an abused mother, to upbraid an abominable father, to be the homemaker for herself, to police the nightmare relationship between her father and mother:

> I try not to leave her by herself with him. Not even when they are both asleep in the bed. My baby crib is still up in their bedroom so when I hear them at night I throw a fit and will not stop until I can sleep in the baby bed. He will think twice when I am around.

After her mother commits suicide with an overdose of heart pills, Old Ellen rides to the funeral and is not deceived:

> The undertaker opens the car door for me. He has been to the house twice since Sunday just to say he

cares. I am glad he cares but I think I would like him better if he said it is my job to care. I make more money than you will ever see just to care. That would not offend me.

Whew. The girl with the x-ray eyes. Not since the poetry of Emily Dickinson do we remember such an unblinking stare. That would not offend me, she says; truth does not offend Old Ellen. But like Hamlet, she sees great offense in lies.

Walker Percy described Ellen Foster as a southern Holden Caulfield, and we can see why. Like Salinger's character from *Catcher in the Rye*, Ellen narrates her own story in her own colloquial voice. Like Holden, she is telling the story later, through recollections. Like Holden, she has been severely hurt and is trying to heal. Like Holden, she has had a miserable experience being the child of her parents. Like Holden, she is too old, too jaded, too ironic, too skeptical, too world-wise. Like Holden, she uses the word *old* as an epithet; remember Holden's Old Jane, Old Phoebe, Old Sally, Old Allie, Old Eustacia? Like Holden, she hates, and sees right through, phonies, but she can still view phoniness with a saving sense of humor:

Dora has soaked the seat of this car. My daddy is not aware of this but I am so I slide closer to the window to put some space between this red suit and Dora. Old as me and wets herself once or twice a day. I know they expect this dress back dry. Dora's mama would stand beside Dora dripping and deny her big girl wet herself.

You are right, Aunt Nadine. I promise never to pee in your girl's pants again.

And like Holden, Ellen has a characteristic language that is identifiable, that we recognize as her voice. Reading *Catcher in the Rye*, we become accustomed to Holden's words: phonies, that kills me, Old Ackley, I'm not kidding, if you want to know the truth, corny, and vulgarities. Ellen too has her signature: Old Ellen, my mama's mama, my new mama, my own self, the indefinite article for the definite article (a egg sandwich), southern cliches—and euphoric descriptions of ordinary food that only a child who knows hunger would think of:

> There is a plenty to eat here and if we run out of something we just go to the store and get some more. I had me a egg sandwich for breakfast, mayonnaise on both sides. And I may fix me another one for lunch.

So there. Aren't you impressed? Mayonnaise on both sides. And just imagine, she may have another one for lunch. Our hearts break, and we have only read two pages of the novel.

Ellen's background of poverty has left other marks on her. She does not even know the names of common household appliances such as vacuum cleaners or dish washers, which she describes as things:

> My new mama lays out the food and we all take a turn to dish it out. Then we eat and have a good time. Toast or biscuits with anything you please. Eggs any style....I keep my elbows off the table and wipe my mouth like a lady....When everybody is done eating my new mama puts the dishes in a thing, shuts the door, cuts it on, and Wa-La they are clean.

Wa-La. Ellen's poverty has impoverished her language, and it is only gradually that we realize how intelligent she is. She buys herself a microscope and studies paramecia, diatoms, and euglenas. More than Scout Finch who taught herself to read, and Holden who adored *The Return of the Native*, Ellen has a personal relationship with books. She cherishes a set of encyclopedias that has a photograph of a "froze" sneeze, and has developed a taste in literature that is far beyond her chronological age:

> Lately I lay up in the bed and read old books. I told the library teacher I wanted to read everything of some count so she made me a list. That was two years ago and I'm up to the Brontë sisters now. I do not read comic books or the newspaper. I find out what news I need off the television.
> I can hardly tolerate the stories we read for school. Cindy or Lou with the dog or cat.

Go ahead, wince, and then I will continue the passage.

> Cindy or Lou with the dog or cat. Always setting out on some adventure. They might meet a bandit or they might hop a freight but the policeman or the engineer always brings them home and they are still good children.
> I myself prefer the old stories. When I started my project I enjoyed the laughing Middle Ages lady that wore red boots. She was on a trip with a group of people swapping stories, carrying on, slapping each other on the back.

We can only laugh at Ellen's description of Chaucer's

Wife of Bath. When she tries to convince her cousin Dora that she has a boyfriend, she relies on literature to provide the name:

Dora just said ha! I didn't know you had a boyfriend.
Well I do!
I've never seen you with one at school. I can see everything you do at recess and lunch time....I don't believe you.
Well it is true I told her hard.
OK then. What's his name?
Nick Adams is who I would have picked out to love if it was up to me so I said his name as honest as I could. I figured I was safe with him because of Dora's reading habits.
He doesn't go to our school. You're making him up!

Nick Adams. She would have picked out to love Nick Adams, Ernest Hemingway's broken boy who retreated to the safe solitude of the cold trout stream, where the terrors of self-interpretation could be lost in the sound of the rippling water and the memories of injuries could be replaced with the simple tasks of fishing. Alone.

Here we see a character through the eyes of a character, as we did when Holden loved Hardy's Eustacia Vye, and we reflect that Ellen is in the fifth grade.

We never know Ellen's real name. Foster is the name she chooses for herself, when she goes to live with her self-chosen foster mother. By the time her story starts, she shakes chronically, her parents are dead, her grandmother (whom she can only bring herself to call "my mama's mama") has treated her cruelly and died, her aunt and cousin have coldly furnished her with a heartbreaking

Christmas, and she has, like Jane Eyre, launched herself out, an escapee, struggling for survival in a world that is giving her precious little support.

But as by some miracle, she lands in the home of her new mama, her foster mother, who does accept her and give her, finally, the love she needs so desperately. Arriving on Christmas day, she offers her new mama one hundred and sixty-six dollars that she has saved as payment for letting her live there. But her new mama is not interested in the money:

> I can't take this money. I tell you what. I'm going to call County Social Services first thing in the morning and we'll get the ball rolling. I can't promise you anything but if you need a place as badly as it appears then we would welcome you here.
>
> That sounded a little bit like something from one of my old books but I had waited so long to believe somebody that I just listened and believed.
>
> And then she hugged me. She leaned over me and pulled me up next to her and it was just like I wanted it to be.

It makes us cry. Reading this, we are grateful for Ellen's survival, and we are thankful to her new mama for taking her in, but we know that it is Ellen who has saved herself—through her determination, through her control of her own goodness, through her courage in facing many unknowns, and through her resourceful intelligence.

When Ellen wants to give her aunt Nadine and her cousin Dora Christmas presents, she decides to give them her own paintings but chooses paintings of cats, knowing that they would not like the paintings she prefers:

They could use some art on the wall even if it is the copied kind. I do not think they would go for one of my experimental pictures or the one I call brooding ocean.

So they get some fuzzy cats. They do not take long to paint but if you do not know a thing about art it will look to you like it took me forever. Then I sign my name Ellen swirly at the edge of a paw. It looks good but it is not something I would have in my own house. But just as long as they like it.

It do not think they even know I have that talent. Won't that be a surprise!

I would really like to paint them one of my brooding oceans but they would miss the point I am sure of how the ocean looks strong and beautiful and sad at the same time and that is really something if you think about it. They would not like the picture because it looks so evil when you first look at it. It is not something that would grow on them. Not like these cats hopping around teasing with a ball of yarn. I like that picture fine except once you look at it one time you have seen and felt everything you will ever see and feel about those cats.

The theme of Ellen's personality is perhaps indicated by the quotation from Ralph Waldo Emerson's inscription to "Self-Reliance" that Kaye Gibbons presents at the beginning of the novel:

Cast the bantling on the rocks,
Suckle him with the she-wolf's teat,
Wintered with the hawk and fox,
Power and speed be hands and feet.

Yes, self-reliance. The poet John Berryman once wrote in a poem, ever to complain that you're bored, means you have no inner resources. Ellen Foster has enormous inner resources, and she has discovered them. Though she is hurt, she is pushing herself forward through her life. She still believes that "I am not exactly a vision. But Lord I have good intentions that count." She is, despite her relief at finding her new mama, a mama to herself. She is her own foster self. This inner self-reliance, and her confidence in its truth and strength, will get her past the dangers that still await her, and will help her heal. She will become an adult version of the eleven-year-old fifth grader whose words we read, a woman of remarkable presence, of remarkable self. And this self will continue to glow with her luminous intelligence that makes us smile with affection and draws us toward her:

It was winter then and I had all but quit going to school. I kept expecting the police to come after me but they never did. If I failed tests the days I did show up then they might have punished me but I never missed spelling words and the numbers I did wrong were careless errors.

I always thought I would have more fun going to a harder school.

THIRTEEN

The Scarlet Letter

Nathaniel Hawthorne

Amid the frosty peaks of American literature is one rocky summit whose profile is especially eminent against the thin oxygen of the upper atmosphere. It is a jagged peak, swept by the iciest of winds. Its environment is pure, silent, and harsh.

Upon first glance, the freezing truth of Nathaniel Hawthorne's *The Scarlet Letter* is apparent. Here are the first words:

THE PRISON DOOR

A throng of bearded men, in sad-colored garments and gray, steeple-crowned hats, intermixed with women, some wearing hoods, and others bareheaded, was assembled in front of a wooden edifice, the door of which was heavily timbered with oak and studded with iron spikes.

A tougher sentence has rarely been seen. It might be a sentence from a modern, dingy, Orwell novel or a futuristic Macintosh advertisement, attacking the dogmatic conformism of IBM. But Hawthorne is using his sentence to shock us and alienate us from the cruel prison of society, with its oaken, spiked doors of judgment, its condemnation of individuality, its iron-spiked rules and its steeple-crowned restrictions on creative life and freedom of mind.

In these first words, Hawthorne brings his immense art to bear, fusing sound and idea and transgressing the false dichotomy of prose and poetry. His description of the crowd and prison is filled with ponderous, harsh sounds that pound, stab, and scar:

> A throng of bearded men, in sad-colored garments and gray, steeple-crowned hats, intermixed with women, some wearing hoods, and others bareheaded, was assembled in front of a wooden edifice, the door of which was heavily timbered with oak and studded with iron spikes.

It is the poetic equivalent of a beating, with the bludgeoning *b*s, *g*s, and *d*s and the spiked, *k*-sounding consonants *c*, *k*, and *x*. These harsh consonants are conveyed on an undercurrent of bass vowels, the sad and low murmur of *throng, crowned, hoods, others, front, wooden, door, oak*, and *studded*, that propel the sentence to its last incongruous sound, *spikes*.

Yikes. The language is hostile with formality. The prison is not a building; it is an edifice, the door of which is heavily timbered. The men are intermixed with the women. The crowd is assembled. The clothing is garments. The colors are gray and sad, the door is oak, and the last word is *spikes*.

Yikes. In case we have no brains, Hawthorne spells out his intent in the next paragraph by describing "the black flower of civilized society, a prison."

Hmm, wethinks, perhaps this is not a pulp romance.

The black flower of civilized society, the prison, is immediately contrasted by an image of the "deep heart of Nature," a wild rose, and it is not, let us note, inside the prison:

But on one side of the portal, and rooted almost at the threshold, was a wild rosebush, covered, in this month of June, with its delicate gems, which might be imagined to offer their fragrance and fragile beauty to the prisoner as he went in, and to the condemned criminal as he came forth to his doom, in token that the deep heart of Nature could pity and be kind to him.

The wild rosebush, fragile, fragrant, and beautiful, is a symbol of pity and kindness, a stark contrast with the "grim rigidity that petrified the bearded physiognomies of these good people." Good, Hawthorne means, in their own steeple-crowned self-congratulations.

Upon this stage of prison and rosebush walks Hester Prynne who has borne a child in the absence of Mister Prynne and who must now stand on a public scaffold, receiving the disapprobation and ostracism of the entire community, and of whom is demanded the name of her fellow sinner, the father of the child Pearl.

This being *The Scarlet Letter*, you know the rest. The community pillar who publicly demands the sinner's name is, of course, the sinner himself: the Reverend Arthur Dimmesdale. And at the back of the assembled throng of hooded and steeple-crowned heads is, of course, Mister Prynne himself, aka Old Roger Chillingworth. Arthur demands, Hester shakes her head no, she and Rog recognize each other, Rog follows her to prison where he too demands to know the sinner's name, she refuses him too, he vows to discover the sinner through his own devices, and the hunt is on. Eventually, Roger discovers Arthur, torments him by irritating his conscience, foils Hester and Arthur's scheme to escape on a ship, and watches as Arthur dies in public confession, evading at last Chillingworth-Prynne's bony clutches. In the coda, Hester returns and finishes her life in the scene of her defining deeds, and Pearl is thought to be far away, married, and happy.

Melodrama, says you.

Yes, says I, but melodrama with a twist. What makes the saccharine sounds of bad organ accompaniment abate is Hawthorne's fix on character. Oh, the dim force of the tremulous Dimmesdale is worth noting, and the chilling intent of Old Roger Chillingworth is interesting, but what really attracts the mind to Hawthorne's story is not these men, but the women: Hester and Pearl.

Hester and her daughter are two alter egos in a pod— brilliant, stubborn, and individualistic. Whether they are staunchly individualistic, as the cliché requires, is a matter of dispute, but they are clearly flowers that grow outside the oaken wall of society.

Hester, although she "came to have a part to perform in the world," with her native energy and "rare capacity," felt isolated, marginal, and different:

> In all her intercourse with society, however, there was nothing that made her feel as if she belonged to it. Every gesture, every word, and even the silence of those with whom she came in contact, implied, and often expressed, that she was banished, and as much alone as if she inhabited another sphere...

In time, the effect of this ostracism and outcast identity was to diminish Hester's feeling of womanhood.

> If she survive, the tenderness will either be crushed out of her, or—and the outward semblance is the same—crushed so deeply into her heart that it can

never show itself more....She who has once been woman, and ceased to be so, might at any moment become a woman again, if there were only the magic touch to effect the transfiguration.

Perhaps as a consequence of this sublimation of tenderness, Hester's mind averts its vision from the wonted mundane matters to others more philosophical: "her life had turned, in a great measure, from passion and feeling to thought."

To thought. And when one turns to thought in an age of reason, and especially in a condition of isolation, devoid of the normal converse that tethers us to the views of our companions, any thought can happen. Hester is no longer chained to the minds of her community:

> ...she cast away the fragments of a broken chain. The world's law was no law for her mind. It was an age in which the human intellect, newly emancipated, had taken a more active and a wider range than for many centuries before. Men of the world had overthrown nobles and kings. Men bolder than these had overthrown and rearranged—not actually, but within the sphere of theory, which was their real abode— the whole system of ancient prejudice, wherewith was linked much of ancient principle. Hester Prynne imbibed this spirit. She assumed a freedom of speculation, then common enough on the other side of the Atlantic, but which our forefathers, had they known it, would have held to be a deadlier crime than that stigmatized by the scarlet letter. In her lonesome cottage by the seashore, thoughts visited her, such as dared to enter no other dwelling in New England; shadowy guests that would have been as perilous as

demons to their entertainer, could they have been seen so much as knocking at her door.

What thoughts?
We get one clear glimpse. When Hester urges Dimmesdale to leave Boston, to flee down the forest path and escape, her full power comes briefly into view:

"Is the world, then, so narrow?" exclaimed Hester Prynne, fixing her deep eyes on the minister's and instinctively exercising a magnetic power over a spirit so shattered and subdued that it could hardly hold itself erect. "Doth the universe lie within the compass of yonder town, which only a little time ago was but a leaf-strewn desert, as lonely as this around us? Whither leads yonder forest track? Backwards to the settlement, thou sayest! Yes; but onward, too! Deeper it goes, and deeper, into the wilderness, less plainly to be seen at every step! until, some few miles hence, the yellow leaves will show no vestige of the white man's tread. There thou art free!". . . . . .

Hawthorne tells us little more.
But in her emancipated freedom of speculation, not grounded in passion and feeling but thought, Hester plays a singular role in literary history, far from the domestic and romantic travails of Emma Bovary, Eustacia Vye, or Elizabeth Bennet. Hester is a character of striking individuality, and striking mind.
And the one person from whom she is not isolated, not estranged, is her daughter Pearl.
Pearl is more than a chip off the old block. She is an extrusion and extension of Hester's most unique qualities. She is Hester, amplified.

Our first encounter with Pearl comes as Hester stands, with Pearl in her arms, on the scaffold in ignominy, facing the rebuke of the crowd and listening to her paramour ask for the name of her paramour. As dim Dad leans down from the balcony in tremulous irony, demanding the truth, Pearl responds to her father's voice, intuitively baby-bonding with its genetically familiar rhythms:

> The young pastor's voice was tremulously sweet, rich, deep, and broken. The feeling that it so evidently manifested, rather than the direct purport of the words, caused it to vibrate within all hearts, and brought the listeners into one accord of sympathy. Even the poor baby at Hester's bosom was affected by the same influence, for it directed its hitherto vacant gaze towards Mr. Dimmesdale, and held up its little arms, with a half pleased, half plaintive murmur.

Precocious child. Her instinctive reach for her father tips us off at the story's inception. We feel a rush of it-can't-be, oh-you're-kidding incredulity, but we know in our hearts that Good Reverend Dimmesdale is Pearl's secret father and that he and Hester are in Big Trouble.

Gradually, we learn more about Pearl. Under Hester's care, she grows into a beautiful child. She has "no physical defect," has "natural dexterity," and possesses a "native grace." Her physical beauty is complemented by "a trait of passion" and a "certain depth of hue." She has an "outward mutability" and depth, "as well as variety." These characteristics might belong to any small, stubborn child, but Pearl's nature extends further:

> The child could not be made amenable to rules. In giving her existence, a great law had been broken,

and the result was a being whose elements were perhaps beautiful and brilliant, but all in disorder; or with an order peculiar to themselves, amidst which the point of variety and arrangement was difficult or impossible to be discovered.

And Pearl's idiosyncratic disorder is only the beginning; her emotional center is a projection of her mother's defiance and fierce adherence to her own definitions of right and wrong.

Above all, the warfare of Hester's spirit, at that epoch, was perpetuated in Pearl. [Hester] could recognize her wild, desperate, defiant mood, the flightiness of her temper, and even some of the very cloud-shapes of gloom and despondency that had brooded in her heart.

This wild, desperate child—who cannot be made amenable to rules, who has a "remarkable precocity and acuteness," whose mental arrangement is difficult or impossible to be discovered, who is despondent, defiant, and flighty—at times seems not even human:

Brooding over all these matters, the mother felt like one who has evoked a spirit, but, by some irregularity in the process of conjuration, has failed to win the master-word that should control this new and incomprehensible intelligence.

This new and incomprehensible intelligence...it is no wonder that Pearl is unable to intermix—isn't that Hawthorne's word?—with other children. But precocious Pearl is an island universe, and the other children can sense it:

> How soon—with what strange rapidity, indeed!—
> did Pearl arrive at an age that was capable of social
> intercourse, beyond the mother's ever-ready smile
> and nonsense words! And then what a happiness
> would it have been, could Hester Prynne have heard
> her clear, birdlike voice mingling with the uproar of
> other childish voices, and have distinguished and
> unravelled her own darling's tones, amid all the
> entangled outcry of a group of sportive children!
> But this could never be. Pearl was a born outcast of
> the infantile world...Nothing was more remarkable
> than the instinct, as it seemed, with which the child
> comprehended her loneliness; the destiny that had
> drawn an inviolable circle round about her; the whole
> peculiarity, in short, of her position in respect to other
> children.

In Pearl her mother recognizes an "ever creative
spirit," "a state of preternatural activity," and most
poignantly, a "constant recognition of an adverse world."
And these qualities increase with time. As Pearl grows,
her perceptions and expressions become stronger. She
becomes attached to the scarlet letter on her mother's
bosom and becomes obsessed with peculiarities of her
anonymous father: Why does the minister keep his hand
over his heart? Why does the minister speak to us alone
but never in public?

Why? Why? Why? This young, "incomprehensible
intelligence," this incipient being who develops with a
"strange rapidity," who defies her mother's commands
and answers saucily to the Governor himself, has a mind of
her own. When Hester learns that Governor Bellingham

intends to take Pearl away and have her raised in a decent home, she leads Pearl to the Governor's house at once in order to plead for her right to keep her daughter. As they approach, Pearl gives another indication of her luminous intelligence:

> Pearl, looking at this bright wonder of a house, began to caper and dance, and imperatively required that the whole breadth of sunshine should be stripped off its front, and given her to play with.

Perhaps, like Peter Pan's shadow, a sheet of sunshine can be folded and put in a drawer, but the technique for doing so is yet to be perfected. Hester tells imperious Pearl to gather her own sunshine.

When Governor Bellingham puts Pearl to the test and asks her Who Made Thee, she responds with all the pride and defiance that she possesses:

> ...the child finally announced that she had not been made at all, but had been plucked by her mother off the bush of wild roses that grew by the prison door.

And in metaphorical terms, Pearl is right. She is not a product of the steeple-crowned people and their iron-spiked prisons; she is a product of the wild rose bush, an expression of the deep heart of Nature, growing outside the walls.

When Governor Bellingham rebuffs Hester, she turns desperately to the honorable Dimmesdale for protection, entreating him to speak for her; he convinces Bellingham that Hester should keep the child, but the effort exhausts him, and he slinks to the side of the room, "tremulous with the vehemence of his appeal."

Pearl, that wild and flighty little elf, stole softly towards him, and taking his hand in the grasp of both of her own, laid her cheek against it; a caress so tender, and withal so unobtrusive, that her mother, who was looking on, asked herself, "Is that my Pearl?"

It is perhaps the best moment that Pearl and her father ever share. Soon, he will be gone, but not before he redeems Pearl's isolation from humanity by publicly confessing and claiming her and her mother at his death scene. Atop the scaffold where Hester's shame was made public, Chillingworth asks Pearl to give him a kiss, though she had previously washed his first kiss off in a brook. This time, she is ready:

Pearl kissed his lips. A spell was broken. The great scene of grief, in which the wild infant bore a part, had developed all her sympathies; and as her tears fell upon her father's cheek, they were the pledge that she would grow up amid human joy and sorrow, nor forever do battle with the world, but be a woman in it.

In his final act, Chillingworth has restored his daughter to the human race. And she, perhaps, is not the only beneficiary; Pearl will receive the inheritance of Old Roger Chillingworth, Mrs. Prynne's lawful Mister. Why he leaves Pearl his money, only he could say, but the unlikely inheritance makes Pearl the "richest heiress of her day" and adjusts the sternness of public opinion before Hester, and her child, disappear. Later, Hester returns, still wearing her scarlet letter on her breast, but Pearl has vanished forever. Somewhere, however, she must live on, for Hester's old age is attended by intriguing contacts from afar:

> But, through the remainder of Hester's life, there were indications that the recluse of the scarlet letter was the object of love and interest with some inhabitant of another land. Letters came, with armorial seals upon them, though of bearing unknown to English heraldry. In the cottage there were articles of comfort and luxury, such as Hester never cared to use, but which only wealth could have purchased, and affection have imagined for her. There were trifles, too, little ornaments, beautiful tokens of a continual remembrance, that must have been wrought by delicate fingers at the impulse of a fond heart.

And so Pearl, the wild child, the demon girl of Boston, allows her incomprehensible intelligence to mature into caring and stable adulthood, where, we hope, her extraordinary qualities bloom into the inherent benefits of a brilliant, creative, and energetic mind, and where her individuality and independence do not become the stuff of tragedy, as they did for her mother.

And what of her mother?

In the end, Hester reverses the polarity of her scarlet symbol, transforming it from a stigma of shame into a badge of concern, and the black walls of the prison come tumbling down. Suddenly, we remember that after all, the rose bush was never so far from the prison portal. In a sense, Hester makes peace with society and gives to others the benefits of her years of pain:

> ...people brought all their sorrows and perplexities and besought her counsel, as one who had herself

gone through a mighty trouble. Women, more especially—in the continually recurring trials of wounded, wasted, wronged, misplaced, or erring and sinful passion—or with the dreary burden of a heart unyielded, because unvalued and unsought—came to Hester's cottage, demanding why they were so wretched, and what the remedy! Hester comforted and counselled them, as best she might. She assured them, too, of her firm belief, that, at some brighter period, when the world should have grown ripe for it, in Heaven's own time, a new truth would be revealed, in order to establish the whole relation between man and woman on a surer ground of mutual happiness.

Is the relation between man and woman on a surer ground of mutual happiness today? Who can say, despite our sociologies and statistical studies? There are surely revengeful Chillingworths, tremulous Dimmesdales, and self-determining Hester Prynnes in abundance now, but there are also extraordinary Pearls of incomprehensible intelligence. Must these new Pearls bear a stigma, scarlet or otherwise, for their strange rapidity, their flightiness, or their demands to hold the sunshine? Or can we understand them, appreciate them, teach them, and help them live out the promise in their precious qualities before they, too, depart for a far off place?

FOURTEEN

The Adventures of Huckleberry Finn

Mark Twain

What would Samuel Clemens think of his book now? In 1884, when this prototypical American classic was first published, the book must have had a different feel. The Civil War was still a living memory, many Americans had lived as slaves during part of their lifetimes, American English had not evolved its modern alternatives for the language of race, and a book that used the word nigger on every page could still seem innocent.

Today, *The Adventures of Huckleberry Finn* presents reading challenges never envisioned by Mark Twain. We feel stung by the racist language and repulsed by the superficial stereotyping of Jim and other African-Americans in the story, and our ability to sink into the story and enjoy its adventure and humor is constantly disrupted by these linguistic violations of our modern democratic mores.

Whatever its merits, what are the risks involved in having young people read *Huckleberry Finn*? Is it still suitable for personal or classroom reading for secondary students? Does it have overriding merits or even counteracting inner truths that detoxify the poisonous effect of its language?

These are difficult questions, and I will tell you now that I can not answer them all to my own satisfaction. There is a part of me, and of many of us, that wants simply to ostracize books with such language, period. Not ban them or remove them from library shelves, but not personally read them or assign them to impressionable students. I would not, for example, consider showing the film *Birth of a Nation* in my class, regardless of its status as a pioneering work in film history.

But I am no book banner.

And *The Adventures of Huckleberry Finn* is no ordinary book. It is a difficult dilemma, to choose between stomaching intolerable language and abandoning *Huckleberry Finn*, but choose we must, so it is well to review both the book and our own hearts periodically, that our foundations are firm.

Perhaps the first question to ask in reevaluating the place of *Huckleberry Finn* in a modern curriculum is, are there other severe difficulties with the book, or is its racially offensive language the only problem? If Twain had worked around the language, would anyone today wish to reject the book?

It is difficult to think so. The saga of Huck and Jim together on a raft in the Mississippi River, with the rich cast of characters they encounter on the journey, has become a literary symbol for the American experience. It is a journey through America, though the heart of its landscape, and through the heart of its population.

And of course, *The Adventures of Huckleberry Finn* is a significant work of literary art. Ernest Hemingway said that all modern American literature was based on this book, and we can see why. It is difficult to imagine, for example, J.D. Salinger writing *Catcher in the Rye* if Mark Twain had not first broken the barriers of propriety and written an entire novel in the illiterate language of the town drunkard's kid. What a shock it must have been to readers, whose every previous book had been narrated in perfect English, to turn to the first page of *Huckleberry*

Finn and read:

> You don't know about me without you have read a
> book by the name of *The Adventures of Tom Sawyer*;
> but that ain't no matter.

Ye gods: *without, ain't,* a double negative—a catastrophe.
And that is only the beginning. On the same page, we
read that "Tom and me found the money," that "She put
me in them new clothes," and that "Aunt Polly...and
Mary, and the Widow Douglas is all told about." The
skin positively crawls: object pronouns as subjects of
verbs, singular verbs for plural subjects, object pronouns
for demonstrative adjectives.

But the Rubicon was crossed; Twain had reached the
other side: The anonymous narrator with perfect English
had vanished, a whole book was narrated within the
mind of an ignorant, illiterate protagonist, and literature
would never go back.

Of course the limitations of Huckleberry's language
were not the limits of Twain's. The crude veneer of
solecisms and illiteracy in *The Adventures of Huckleberry
Finn* is deceiving; this pseudobumpkin's book mes-
merizes the reader, concealing a host of satires and
allusions to other literature and philosophy, although,
for example, there are direct references to *Hamlet, Don
Quixote,* and Sir Walter Scott, we are still surprised to
come upon a spoof of Plato, incongruously rendered in
the colloquy between Huck and Jim. Huck says:

> "S'pose a man was to come to you and say Polly-
> voo-franzy—what would you think?"
> "I wouldn' think nuffn; I'd take en bust him over
> de head....I wouldn't 'low [nobody] to call me dat."

"Shucks, it ain't calling you anything. It's only saying, do you know how to talk French?"

"Well, den, why couldn't he say it?"

"Why, he is a-saying it. That's a Frenchman's way of saying it."

"Well, it's a blame ridicklous way, en I doan' want to hear no mo' 'bout it. Dey ain' no sense in it."

"Looky here, Jim; does a cat talk like we do?"

"No, a cat don't."

"Well, does a cow?"

"No, a cow don't nuther."

"Does a cat talk like a cow, or a cow talk like a cat?"

"No, dey don't."

"It's natural and right for 'em to talk different from each other, ain't it?"

"Course."

"And ain't it natural and right for a cat and a cow to talk different from us?"

"Why, mos' sholy it is."

"Well, then, why ain't it natural and right for a Frenchman to talk different from us? You answer me that."

But Jim is not dismayed by Huck's dialogue; there is a bit of Socrates in him, too, and he turns the table:

"Is a cat a man, Huck?"

"No."

"Well, den, day ain't no sense in a cat talkin' like a man. Is a cow a man?—er is a cow a cat?"

"No, she ain't either of them."

"Well, den, she ain't got no business to talk like either one er the yuther of 'em. Is a Frenchman a man?"

"Yes."

"Well, den! Dad blame it, why doan' he talk like a man? You answer me dat!"

The Platonic style is unmistakable, but the transformation is hilarious. We see the familiar step-by-step method of disclosing the truth, but the language is completely unsophisticated, the concepts are convoluted, and the examples are ludicrous: "Does a cat talk like a cow?" So much for the Socratic method.

And Plato is not the only mind to become the object of Twain's humor. Later, when Jim is captured, and Tom Sawyer shows up, he and Huck make plans to rescue Jim from captivity and set him free, even though in their benighted minds both of them regard their act as stealing property and feel that they are doing wrong. Rejecting the obvious, that they could just open the door and let Jim out, Tom asks what they can use to dig under the wall and free Jim. Huck suggests the picks and shovels in the adjacent storage room, but Tom will not have it:

"Huck Finn, did you ever hear of a prisoner having picks and shovels, and all the modern conveniences in his wardrobe to dig himself out with? Now I want to ask you—if you got any reasonableness in you at all—what kind of a show would that give him to be a hero? Why, they might as well lend him the key and done with it. Picks and shovels—why, they wouldn't furnish 'em to a king."

"Well, then," I says, "if we don't want the picks and shovels, what do we want?"

"A couple of case-knives."

"To dig the foundations out from under that cabin

with?"

"Yes."

"Confound it, it's foolish, Tom."

"It don't make no difference how foolish it is, it's the right way—and it's the regular way. And there ain't no other way, that ever I heard of, and I've read all the books that gives any information about these things. They always dig out with a case-knife—and not through dirt, mind you; generly it's through solid rock."

Tom's intractable romanticism, his refusal to compromise, and his obsession with the books suddenly remind us of the other great character in literature to be so obsessed and foolish at the same time, Don Quixote. Tom is Don Quixote as a child, smiting the foes and standing for the right. Just as we ask ourselves whether Mark Twain could have intentionally modeled Tom after Don Quixote, we recall the scene from the beginning of *Huckleberry Finn* in which Tom forms a gang and leads his fearless gangsters in an attack against Spaniards and A-rabs, only to have the gang members complain, in Huck's words, that "It warn't anything but a Sunday-school picnic, and only a primer class at that. We busted it up, and chased the children up the hollow." Undaunted, Tom accuses the other boys of blindness:

I didn't see no di'monds, and I told Tom Sawyer so. He said there was loads of them there, anyway; and he said there was A-rabs there, too, and elephants and things. I said, why couldn't we see them, then? He said if I warn't so ignorant, but had read a book called *Don Quixote*, I would know without asking. He said it was all done by enchantment. He said there was hundreds of soldiers there, and elephants and treasure, and so on, but we had enemies which he called magicians, and they had turned the whole thing into an infant Sunday-School, just out of spite. I said, all right; then the thing for us to do was to go for the magicians. Tom Sawyer said I was a numskull.

Images come to mind of Huck, Jim, and Don Quixote floating down the Mississippi, while Sancho Panza scoots along the muddy bank on his burro, crying "Wait boss, wait boss!" And what trouble would Tom and Don get into, forgetting for a moment that Don is a title and not a name, if they were to set off together with no realist Huck or Sancho to keep them from disaster? The Tom and Don Show. We can see the appeal that Cervantes's immortal character had for Mark Twain; Don Quixote is the *locus classicus* for the character who always does the right thing—with complete disregard for its practicality, its advantage to himself, and its safety. Villain dead ahead; Charge! The pure righter of wrongs, the rescuer of the innocent, the defender of his Lady, the smiter of Philistines, the uncompromising romantic idealist. Don Quixote's adherence to his beliefs is so rare that the character seems ludicrous and is depicted as insane to seem credible. Imagine the mundane world's reaction to such a real person, who would never sit silent, who would always speak up against unfairness, who would tolerate no injustice, who would make every wave and upset every apple cart in the name of Right. The world would not understand, but Tom Sawyer would.

Plato, Cervantes, and what about Freud? It is tempting, later in the story, to think that Twain is spoofing the theories of Sigmund Freud, whose *Die Traumdeutung* or *Interpretation of Dreams*, founded our modern ideas about the nature of the mind. When Huck and Jim get separated in the fog, Huck gets back to the raft to find Jim asleep and convinces Jim that they were never separated at all, and Jim has only been dreaming. Huck asks Jim about his dream:

> ...he said he must start in and "'terpret" it, because it was sent for a warning. He said the first towhead stood for a man that would try to do us some good, but the current was another man that would get us away from him. The whoops was warnings that would come to us every now and then, and if we didn't try hard to make out to understand them they'd just take us into bad luck, 'stead of keeping us out of it.

Had *The Adventures of Huckleberry Finn* been written in 1914, rather than in 1884, this passage might have been a knowing spoof of Freud's ideas, but *The Interpretation of Dreams* was not published until 1900, and so the passage is only uncannily prescient.

A knowing nod to other literature is not the only interesting quality in *The Adventures of Huckleberry Finn*. There are times when Twain's language, even through the rough medium of Huckleberry's mind, is beautifully poetic. The first pages of the nineteenth chapter should be read aloud, softly, and to those who have their eyes closed. "Two or three days and nights went by," it begins, and paragraph after beautiful paragraph describes the life on the water. In these passages, Twain controls the sound of the words, the rhythm:

> Once or twice of a night we would see a steamboat slipping along in the dark, and now and then she would belch a whole world of sparks up out of her

chimbleys, and they would rain down in the river and look awful pretty; then she would turn a corner and her lights would wink out and her powwow shut off and leave the river still again; and by and by her waves would get to us, a long time after she was gone, and joggle the raft a bit, and after that you wouldn't hear nothing for you couldn't tell how long, except maybe frogs or something.

Do you hear them, the waves of the steamboat? And by and by her waves would get to us, and joggle the raft a bit. Anyone who has ever been on a small boat rocked by the wake of another knows this wavy meter. And what about the silence of the semicolon after the words, "still again"? In these passages, we feel the truth of Huck's words, "It's lovely to live on a raft."

Like Swift's Gulliver (Swift finished *Gulliver's Travels* in 1725), Huckleberry reaches adventure after adventure by means of water. Like Gulliver, he gets an eye-full of human frailty and baseness, and like Gulliver, he is often a credulous dupe who is blind to the motivations of people around him. Swift and Twain both used their stories to deplore baseness. Twain, especially, departs from the humorous tone of the tale to show the horror of violence and the blind monstrosity of hatred. At one point Huckleberry finds himself in the middle of a feud between two families, the Grangerfords and the Shepherdsons. With Huckleberry watching from a tree, the Shepherdsons surprise two Grangerford boys in the wooded river bank:

All of a sudden, bang! bang! bang! goes three or four guns—the men had slipped around through the woods and come in from behind without their horses! The boys jumped for the river—both of them hurt—and as they swum down the current the men run along the bank shooting at them and singing out, "Kill them, kill them!" It made me so sick I most fell out of the tree. I ain't a-going to tell all that happened—it would make me sick again if I was to do that. I wished I hadn't ever come ashore that night to see such things. I ain't ever going to get shut of them—lots of times I dream about them.

Nothing funny here—just brutal violence and animal indifference to the value of life. It is an indictment of proclivity for evil. This is tougher stuff than Gulliver's voyage to Liliput, and it is not Twain's only contemptuous moment. His contempt for social superiority is also frequently apparent, as when Huckleberry and Jim share their disgust with the Duke and the Dauphin, and Jim still believes that the two swindlers are genuine royalty:

What was the use to tell Jim these warn't real kings and dukes? It wouldn't 'a' done no good; and, besides, it was just as I said: you couldn't tell them from the real kind.

Twain's irony was not reserved for aristocrats, however. He also despised the vulgar and cowardly mob, as we see when the crowd comes after Sherburn, who has just shot and killed a drunken braggard named Boggs. The crowd swarms up Sherburn's property, whooping like, as Jonathan Swift would have said, yahoos, until Sherburn suddenly comes out of the house:

Just then Sherburn steps out onto the roof of his little front porch, with a double-barrel gun in his hand,

and takes his stand, perfectly ca'm and deliberate, not saying a word. The racket stopped, and the wave sucked back.

Sherburn never said a word—just stood there, looking down. The stillness was awful creepy and uncomfortable. Sherburn ran his eye slowly along the crowd; and wherever it struck the people tried a little to outgaze him, but they couldn't; they dropped their eyes and looked sneaky. Then pretty soon Sherburn sort of laughed; not the pleasant kind, but the kind that makes you feel like when you are eating bread that's got sand in it.

Then he says, slow and scornful:

"The idea of you lynching anybody! It's amusing. The idea of you thinking you had pluck enough to lynch a man! Because you're brave enough to tar and feather poor friendless cast-out women that come along here, did that make you think you had grit enough to lay your hands on a man? Why, a man's safe in the hands of ten thousand of your kind—as long as it's daytime and you're not behind him."

Unquestionably, *The Adventures of Huckleberry Finn* is a rich source of ideas, of literary art, and of insight into both human nature and American nature. Racist language aside, the novel is a high classic of American literature.

But racist language cannot be put aside. What is the relationship of this repulsive language to the inner meaning of the book? Is *Huckleberry Finn* a racist book that will degrade the nation's progress toward egalitarianism? Will *Huckleberry Finn* promote racist thinking in the minds of students? Does the odious surface language manifest a racist meaning? In order to answer these questions, we must consider the nature of

Twain's portrayal of Jim, the elements of Huck and Jim's relationship, the apparent meaning of Huck's benighted attitudes, and the central message of the story. If these things are racist, then the book is racist throughout; if not, then the language might play a different role in the story than one first fears.

Twain's portrayal of Jim is the first clear evidence that the book is not racist in its inner value. Although Jim is ignorant, superstitious, and diffident in ways, he nevertheless emerges as a strong human being, a generous and brave companion, and a caring friend. More than anyone else in the story, Jim lives in deliberate accordance with the Judeo-Christian creed, reflecting to himself that he must do for others what they would do for him. When Tom Sawyer and Huck free Jim, Tom takes a bullet in the leg, and Jim abandons his escape to stay with Tom while Huck goes for help:

> "Well, den, dis is de way it look to me, Huck. Ef it wuz him dat 'uz bein' sot free, en one er ede boys wuz to git shot, would he say, 'Go on en save me, nemmine 'bout a doctor f'r to save dis one'? Is dat like Mars Tom Sawyer? Would he say dat? You bet he wouldn't! Well, den, is Jim gwyne to say it? No, sah—I doan' budge a step out'n dis place 'dout a doctor: not if it's forty year!"

Although Jim repeatedly is left alone with the raft, he always waits for Huck to return, even when waiting might (and eventually does) mean capture and return to slavery. Jim's deep humanity is clear when he considers what he will do with his new freedom:

> Jim talked out loud all the time while I was talking to

myself. He was saying how the first thing he would do when he got to a free state he would go to saving up money and never spend a single cent, and when he got enough he would buy his wife, which was owned on a farm close to where Miss Watson lived; and then they would both work to buy the two children, and if their master wouldn't sell them, they'd get an Ab'litionist to go and steal them.

With this, Twain juxtaposes Huckleberry's obtuse horror that Jim would "steal his children—children that belonged to a man [the slaveowner] I didn't even know; a man that hadn't ever done me no harm." Huckleberry's mind is a case study in the brute stupidity of the proslavery mentality, a mentality that even with his sincere love of Jim he is unable to overcome. The redeeming fact is that even though Huckleberry feels guilty about helping Jim escape and believes he is doing wrong, he nevertheless proceeds to help Jim, deciding that he will risk damnation in order to help his friend.

The relationship between Huck and Jim is a transcending mutual love that takes place in spite of Huck's participation in the racist values that pervade his society. They are friends and confidants; they talk; they share the same ignorant superstitions. Both Huck and Jim wait for each other before shoving off, even when they are desperate to depart. When Huck returns to the raft to find Jim has been captured, not for a second does he consider leaving without Jim; his only thought is what to do next in order to find Jim and set him free.

The central image of *Huckleberry Finn*, the image that artistically and philosophically connects the story's series of events as the act of pilgrimage connects the *Canterbury Tales*, is the image of two Americans, a young black man and a white boy, who journey together in friendship on a small raft down the mighty Mississippi River, working and cooking together, talking together through the long quiet nights, consulting together in times of crisis, taking risks for each other, and rescuing each other alternately as trouble develops. This friendship overcomes all of the odds against it; it overcomes the mercenary racism of the Duke and the Dauphin, the institutionalized racism of the extended society they constantly drift through, and even the internalized racism in Huckleberry's ignorant attitudes that is continually expressed through his detestable language.

In the end, the meaning of *The Adventures of Huckleberry Finn* is one that we should heed, because we are together, all of us, on a very small raft in a very great current, and we too should help each other, wait for each other, and care for each other; the alternative is unthinkable. We know, for as Huck says in the book's last words, we have "been there before."

FIFTEEN

Leaves of Grass

Walt Whitman

If Shakespeare is the Shakespeare of England, and Cervantes is the Shakespeare of Spain, and Hugo is the Cervantes of France, and Homer is the Hugo of Greece, and Goethe is the Hugo of Germany, and Virgil is the Goethe of Rome, and Dante is the Virgil of Italy, and Pushkin is the Dante of Russia, and García Márquez is the Pushkin of our century, then who is the García Márquez of the United States?

Well, is there any immortal literature that has been written in the United States? What literature of ours is definitive, is the prototype of its genre, is the *locus classicus* for a type of literary character, is a landmark in literary art, is on the short list of truly great books of the world? What American writer can withstand being mentioned in the same breath as Dante? As Goethe? As Tolstoy? What American writer is studied in all of the world's great universities and is venerated by writers and poets the world over?

It would be tempting to suggest Mark Twain, and Twain does possess some of these intimations of immortality, but his clouds of glory make thin trails that shrink to insignificance against the great sky of Shakespeare and Goethe. Twain simply was not, for all his appeal and originality, a writer of the necessary magnitude. He lacked...existential power.

It would be tempting, and surely more appropriate, to

suggest Herman Melville. More than his more frequently read friend Hawthorne, Melville contributed a massive, impressive, and philosophically powerful book. *Moby Dick* is without a doubt a work of magnitude, written in a burst of shocking genius, experimental to its bones, and profoundly involved in the basis of life's meaning. *Moby Dick* possesses a little world of immortal characters—Ishmael, Queequeg, and Ahab—and draws its language from an array of other literature, including Shakespeare's *King Lear*. And it would be no certain strike against Melville that *Moby Dick* is a single masterpiece, which Melville was unable to equal in his subsequent works; the same could be said of Cervantes, Hugo, Goethe, Dante, and Tolstoy.

Even the other Shakespeares were no Shakespeare, who was himself the author not only of *Hamlet*, but also of *King Lear*, and *Macbeth*, and *Othello*, *Romeo and Juliet*, *The Tempest*, *The Taming of the Shrew*, *A Midsummer Night's Dream*, *Much Ado About Nothing*, *Julius Caesar*, and many others...any one of which would have made an author immortal.

No, even though his greatness resides in only one book, Melville would be an intelligent nomination for the American Shakespeare.

But even compared to Melville, there is an American literary genius whose work is unique in world literature, far more so than Melville's. After all, Melville did not invent the novel or even revolutionize its form. Melville probed deeply into the souls of his characters, and perhaps deeply into the meaning of existence, but his thinking seems not utterly unlike other ideas we have known. Many authors have explored evil, and fate, and futility. As good as Melville was, there are others like him.

There is no one like Whitman.

For an author of global scope and influence who is a first-magnitude original, whose work is as American as Goethe's is German, whose book is a necessity of life, who is as richly human as Chaucer or Cervantes, who redefined the limits of literary art both in form and in idea, whose thinking continues to have profound importance a century after his death, whose ideas are Dante-vast in scope—for an author like this, American can produce only Whitman.

There is no one—no one at all—like Whitman.

As everyone knows, Emerson was the first to recognize the improbable force of the newcomer Whitman's accomplishment. Emerson wrote to Whitman, congratulating him on "the most extraordinary piece of wit and wisdom that America has yet contributed." Emerson marveled that he had never heard of Whitman before; he knew that such a beginning must have had a long history somewhere.

Of course, it had. Like most of the great creators, Whitman was a voracious reader who loved, among others, Goethe and Sir Walter Scott. And Whitman was a reader of humanity; he was a haunter of locales, an observer of individuals, a converser who stored up, over a period of decades, like a hirsute Jane Goodall recording the behavior of jungle chimps, the multitudinous manifestations of humans being human beings.

Whitman loved people.

Even today, long after generations of Whitman-influenced poets have jaded our ears, and a century of clamor has forced all but the most brow-ridged Neanderthals to affect enlightenment, we still open *Leaves of Grass*, and especially "Song of Myself," with a shock.

My word, Whitman first published this anthem of equality in 1855.

1855.

To get farther ahead of your time than that, you would have to go to someone like, say, Mary Wollstonecraft, whose *Vindication of the Rights of Woman* in 1792 is, well, impossible. It must have been written centuries later by an imposter who foisted a literary fraud off on the unsuspecting literati. Read *Vindication*, and ask yourself who is more advanced: Mary Wollstonecraft, Jane Austen, Charlotte Brontë, or George Eliot.

In 1855 with slavery still in effect and women still denied effective lives, with everyone agreeing that God, the soul, and heaven were good, but humanity, the body, and the world were bad—in this decade before the Civil War, Whitman published the greatest single work of creative optimism in world literature.

Breaking the darkness of Puritanism, Whitman enunciated a poetry of acceptance: acceptance of self, of sex, of both sexes, of the body, of the world, of humanity.

The ghost of Jonathan Edwards, who had told his congregation that the God of Heaven abhorred them and held them over the fires of Hell like loathsome spiders that He wished to drop into the purifying flames, must have sat up in its grave, for with neither warning nor apology, Whitman began his breakout from humanity's self-condemnation:

I celebrate myself, and sing myself,
And what I assume you shall assume,
For every atom belonging to me as good belongs to you.

More revolutionary than Mark Twain's use of

illiterate narration, this was a philosophical shot heard 'round the world. You are not bad, it said. You are not evil or shameful. Your desires are natural. Your body is good. You are lucky to be human and lucky to live in this world of miracles. Like Jesus telling humanity that the poor in spirit are blessed, Whitman identified with all and proclaimed that he was "of the foolish, just as much as the wise."

To women who lived in a rough America, where Man was men and women would not vote in the century, Whitman brought a new truth: "Out of the dimness," Whitman wrote, "opposite equals advance."

Opposite equals.

Advance.

Out of dimness.

More than a century later, these words still bring a chill to our necks. And Whitman did not stop there:

I am the poet of the woman the same as the man,
And I say it is as great to be a woman as to be a man,
And I say there is nothing greater than the mother of men.

To African-Americans free and slave, who lived in an evil society scarcely imaginable today, Whitman brought a new portrayal, not of a cringing stereotype but of a man:

The negro holds firmly the reins of his four horses, the block swags underneath on its tied-over chain,
The negro that drives the long dray of the stone-yard, steady and tall he stands pois'd on one leg on the string-piece,
His blue shirt exposes his ample neck and breast and

loosens over his hip-band,
His glance is calm and commanding, he tosses the slouch of his hat away from his forehead....

To the tired, the poor, the huddled masses yearning to breathe poetry, Whitman brought a new voice of democracy: "I know that the spirit of God is the brother of my own," he wrote, "And that all the men ever born are also my brothers." Moving beyond generality, Whitman identified and described hundreds of men and women: sweet-hearts, old maids, laborers ("And there is no trade or employment but the young man following it may become a hero"), criminals, officers, hospital patients, politicians, and prostitutes. For all, he offered unconditional commiseration:

The prostitute draggles her shawl, her bonnet bobs on her tipsy and pimpled neck,
The crowd laugh at her blackguard oaths, the men jeer and wink to each other,
(Miserable! I do not laugh at your oaths nor jeer you;)

He did not. "Whoever degrades another," Whitman proclaimed, "degrades me." No one, within the word-world of Whitman's poem, would be rejected:

This is the meal equally set, this the meat for natural hunger,
It is for the wicked just the same as the righteous, I make appointments with all,
I will not have a single person slighted or left away,
The kept-woman, sponger, thief, are hereby invited,
The heavy-lipp'd slave is invited, the venerealee is invited;

There shall be no difference between them and the rest.

For words such as these, even in poems, tyrants have dashed brains. But Whitman was undeterred by any threat. "My gait," he announced, "is no fault-finder's or rejecter's gait." For elitists, snobs, and aristocrats of all kinds in all places, Whitman had a new message: "I do not ask who you are, that is not important to me, / You can do nothing and be nothing but what I will infold you."

Nothing.

"And whoever walks a furlong without sympathy," Whitman wrote, "walks to his own funeral drest in his shroud."

These are the Beatitudes of Democracy.

Blessed are the persons.

For theirs is the United States.

Women, Blacks, individuals of all stripes—all were included in the glow of a new acceptance, and Whitman then took his poem deeper, to the structures within the individual, to feelings of shame and bodily self-contempt: "I am the poet of the Body," Whitman said, "and I am the poet of the Soul, / The pleasures of heaven are with me and the pains of hell are with me, / The first I graft and increase upon myself, the latter I translate into a new tongue."

A new tongue for the Body and the Soul: "Lack one lacks both, and the unseen is proved by the seen, / Till that becomes unseen and receives proof in its turn."

A new tongue:

Undrape! you are not guilty to me , nor stale nor discarded,

I see through the broadcloth and gingham whether
or no,
And am around, tenacious, acquisitive, tireless, and
cannot be shaken away.

For Whitman, the body was a miracle: "I cannot
tell how my ankles bend, nor whence the cause of my
faintest wish."

In fact, for Whitman every object and phenomenon
was a miracle:

I believe a leaf of grass is no less than the journey-
work of the stars,
And the pismire is equally perfect, and a grain of
sand, and the egg of the wren,
And the tree-toad is a chef-d'oeuvre for the highest,
And the running blackberry would adorn the parlors
of heaven,
And the narrowest hinge in my hand puts to scorn all
machinery,
And the cow crunching with depress'd head surpasses
any statue,
And a mouse is miracle enough to stagger sextillions
of infidels.

A pismire is an ant, and a *chef-d'oeuvre* is a
masterpiece, and if you think Whitman is exaggerating
about the mouse, consider this experiment: we will have
all nations of the world combine their gross national
products for a decade, and pool the best scientists on the
planet, and give them ten years to build a mouse. If they
fail, they all have to memorize the sermons of Jonathan
Edwards.

Whitman's words are not hyperbole; they are

profoundly visionary. A mouse, or a leaf of grass, or the narrowest hinge in our hand, is infinitely beyond the ability of human science to reproduce. We are surrounded, always and everywhere, by myriad miracles that would stagger sextillions of infidels, but we are so jaded by experience that we are blind to the wonder of the world. We are not as a little child and cannot enter the heaven around us. But Whitman wanted us to see again: "I or you pocketless of a dime," he wrote, "may purchase the pick of the earth."

For a caring reader, *Leaves of Grass* is overwhelming; it is a victorious overcoming, through sheer force of mind and imagination, of cultural limitations that were the product of centuries of Western civilization.

Whitman can be criticized, even ridiculed. In his *Studies in Classic American Literature*, D.H. Lawrence did ridicule Whitman. To Whitman's "I am he that aches of amorous love," Lawrence jeered, "Walter, you are not he. You are just a foolish little Walter." But brilliant critics also have seen the greatness of Whitman. Read Randall Jarrell's discussion of Whitman in his perspicuous *Poetry and the Age*. Perhaps it takes a poet like Jarrell to see the poetry in Whitman's deceptive free verse, but even if we are deaf to the poetry in lines like:

> The carpenter dresses his plank, the tongue of his foreplane whistles its wild ascending lisp

Or:

> The malform'd limbs are tied to the surgeon's table, What is removed drops horribly in a pail

Even if we are deaf to the whistly and wobbly sounds

of these lines, we must still be impressed by the encyclopedic reach of Whitman's imagination.

It might be true that Dante's *Divine Comedy*, especially the *Inferno*, is the greatest single feat of human imagination. The sheer number of Dante's images, the bravery of the attempt (describing Hell?), and the quality of poetic and philosophic power, leave us in literary awe. But Whitman's feat of imagination in *Leaves of Grass* has a similar magnitude and originality. Read carefully through the catalog passages where Whitman enumerates his hosts of individuals, his encyclopedia of vignettes. *Leaves of Grass* is the book in which—more than any other in world literature—one human being deliberately and methodically imagined himself to be everyone else. Swiftly, but with uncanny accuracy, Whitman skims through other people's selves, identifying, sympathizing, understanding, compassionating:

> The little one sleeps in its cradle,
> I lift the gauze and look a long time, and silently brush away flies with my hand.
> The youngster and the red-faced girl turn aside up the bushy hill,
> I peeringly view them from the top.
> The suicide sprawls on the bloody floor of the bedroom,
> I witness the corpse with its dabbled hair, I note where the pistol has fallen.

Or:

> The pedler sweats with his pack on his back, (the purchaser higgling about the odd cent;)
> The bride unrumples her white dress, the minute-

hand of the clock moves slowly,
The opium-eater reclines with rigid head and just-open'd lips,

Or:

The crew of the fish-smack pack repeated layers of halibut in the hold,
The Missourian crosses the plains toting his wares and his cattle

On and on: flatboatmen, patriarchs, coon-seekers, drovers, deck-hands, squaws, marksmen, Yankees, Kentuckians, Californians:

Of every hue and caste am I, of every rank and religion,
A farmer, mechanic, artist, gentleman, sailor, quaker,
Prisoner, fancy-man, rowdy, lawyer, physician, priest.

In no other book has one person so extended the tendrils of his imagination into the lives of all around him, seeing each life through its own eyes, feeling each person through the reality of its own reactions. This effort of Whitman's was not simply spontaneous poetic writing; it was intellectual, poetic, and spiritual and must have taken him years of intense observation and empathy—his family thought he was a bum; all he ever did was stand around and watch, but what watching! Whitman did for humanity what Leonardo did for the phenomena of nature: see. When asked the secret of his art, Leonardo answered *Saper vedere*, to know how to see. Whitman taught himself that in order to see, one must first look, and it was his years of looking that formed the long beginning that Emerson guessed at in his congratulatory letter.

And as we continue to reread Whitman, we are struck by a curious effect: the aura of egotism that seems so salient in our early readings abates and is replaced by a kind of humble serenity and wisdom. "These are really the thoughts of all men in all ages and lands, they are not original with me," he wrote, "If they are not yours as much as mine they are nothing, or next to nothing."

Sometimes the wisdom surprises us with the unrealized obvious:

There was never any more inception than there is now,
Nor any more youth or age than there is now,
And will never be any more perfection than there is now.

Sometimes the wisdom gives us fresh perceptions of our hierarchies:

Have you practis'd so long to learn to read?
Have you felt so proud to get at the meaning of poems?
Stop this day and night with me and you shall possess the origin of all poems.

Sometimes the wisdom combines the love of God with the paradox of Socrates:

A child said What is the grass? fetching it to me with full hands;

How could I answer the child? I do not know what it
is any more than he.
I guess it must be the flag of my disposition, out of
hopeful green stuff woven.
Or, I guess it is the handkerchief of the Lord,
A scented gift and remembrancer designedly dropt,
Bearing the owner's name someway in the corners,
that we may see and remark and say Whose?

In the end, Whitman did not present himself as the
answer or the origin of answers. In the last pages of
"Song of Myself," Whitman emphasized the path of the
individual: "Not I, not any one else can travel that road
for you, / You must travel it for yourself." And: "You are
also asking me questions and I hear you, / I answer that I
cannot answer, you must find out for yourself."
He approached the limits of poetry and comprehension:

There is that in me—I do not know what it is—but
I know it is in me...I do not know it—it is without
name—it is a word unsaid, / It is not in any dictionary,
utterance, symbol...

Even the seemingly invincible limits of logic gave way
to a profounder wisdom:

Do I contradict myself?
Very well then I contradict myself.
(I am large, I contain multitudes.)

"Song of Myself" ends with a simple invitation:
"Failing to fetch me at first keep encouraged, / Missing
me one place search another, / I stop somewhere waiting
for you." Whitman's words are still waiting for us, and

in searching among them, we are perhaps reading the best book, to use Emerson's words, "that America has yet contributed."

SIXTEEN

The Awakening

Kate Chopin

Like Edna Pontellier, the protagonist of Kate Chopin's protofeminist novel *The Awakening*, Kate Chopin was an outsider in Louisiana's Creole society, even though her mother was descended of Creole ancestry. Born Katherine O'Flaherty in 1850, Kate had moved to Louisiana from St. Louis after marrying her Creole husband, Oscar Chopin. And like Edna, Kate Chopin was an independent wife who defied social convention by smoking, going about without the company of her husband, and in other ways living as an iconoclast.

Chopin began writing only after the death of her husband in 1882, when she moved back to St. Louis with her six children. At first, she experienced the rejection that most new authors encounter, but soon her stories were published in magazines such as *The Saturday Evening Post* and *The Atlantic Monthly*. She published her first novel, *At Fault*, at her own expense in 1890 and destroyed her second novel, *Young Dr. Grosse*. When she published her unconventional novel, *The Awakening*, in 1899, a storm of protest arose. *The Awakening* was considered scandalous; like Flaubert's *Madame Bovary*, it offended public decency with its frank portrayal of Edna Pontellier's psychological and sexual independence.

Unlike Flaubert, Kate Chopin was ruined. Her literary career abruptly ended when she could no longer find publishers for her work, and like Thomas Hardy, she quit writing. She died of a cerebral hemorrhage at the age of fifty-three.

Today, Kate Chopin is on every reading list. She wrote few novels but is celebrated for her meticulous descriptions of setting, her precise rendering of dialect, and her objective point of view. *The Awakening* is especially appreciated as an early feminist classic and has taken its place in college surveys of American literature.

Fine, but what are we really to make of this book? Sure, Kate Chopin deserves plaudits for bravery, for challenging the norms and mores that enforced conventional limitations for both novels and women, but it takes more than a brave author to write a classic. Certainly, Kate Chopin deserves recognition for being ahead of her time, for writing a prescient exploration of the free thought and self-direction that women would assume in the future, but it takes more than a forerunner to make a classic, and anyway, Mary Wollstonecraft had brilliantly explored this ground a full century earlier. Chopin was not the mother of feminism.

If this book is to take a permanent place on the shelf, it will have to do it the old-fashioned way, not as a brave attempt or a pioneering beginning, but as a legitimate work of literary art that can stand on its own as a classic novel.

Does Chopin's *The Awakening* do that?

Does it have the artistic quality and the vital substance that are the *sine qua non* of the classic novel? Is it valid to discuss, as a group, *Tom Sawyer*, *The Great Gatsby*, *The Sun Also Rises*, *The Scarlet Letter*, and *The Awakening*?

Yes, perhaps it is.

Scandalous in its *fin de siecle* era, *The Awakening* would raise few eyebrows today, especially as sexuality is concerned. In fact, there is no sexuality in *The*

Awakening, if we refer to descriptions of romantic behavior; the affair that Edna Pontellier has with the young philanderer Arobin is only implied, not described; Chopin's descriptions take us to a first kiss, the chapter fades, and we must infer the rest. Chapter twenty-seven ends with Arobin kissing Edna:

> When he leaned forward and kissed her, she clasped his head, holding his lips to hers.
> It was the first kiss of her life to which her nature had really responded. It was a flaming torch that kindled desire.

And chapter twenty-eight, less than one page long, tells us that Edna cried afterwards, felt the shock of the unaccustomed, and felt as if a mist had been lifted from her eyes, "enabling her to look upon and comprehend the significance of life, that monster made up of beauty and brutality." In Edna's mind, there was neither shame nor remorse, there was only regret that what had led her to the arms of Arobin was not love. It was, as Chopin wrote in an earlier chapter, an "animalism that stirred impatiently within her."

Animalism.

Although we can see why this passage would have seemed scandalous a century ago, it pales beside the routine—we probably should say *de rigueur*—descriptions of physical intimacy that all modern novels seem obliged to contain. One can hardly walk down the supermarket aisles without passing an array of lurid paperbacks in da-glo covers, alluring credulous shoppers into their torrid pages.

No, Kate Chopin was no D.H. Lawrence, boldly leading society to its future physical freedom. Lawrence and other Liberties would have to lead the people.

And perhaps the absence of anything we would regard as daring is an advantage to a modern reader, for failing to find the physical, we find ourselves gazing at the psychological.

And this, surely, is what Kate Chopin intended to write, and did write, about.

Edna Pontellier's path through the pages of The Awakening is, in its most salient aspect, profoundly psychological. As we watch her descend the glidepath to her seemingly inevitable suicide, we see her struggle with layers of internal interpretations; she struggles to understand herself in terms of her location in marriage, in terms of her self-construction as a free woman, and in terms of her existence as a mortal human being.

Edna's marriage to Leonce Pontellier seems designed to self-destruct, designed to awaken independent life in the mordant self that remains to Edna as the novel begins. Leonce is the perfect foil: an egocentric, material, complacent husband who is blind to his blindness, and who understands not the obvious meanings of his actions and statements. As *The Awakening* begins, Leonce is placidly reading the paper, oblivious to the absence of his wife who has had to go to the beach without him. When she returns, it is in the company of a handsome younger man, but Leonce is unperturbed:

> The sunshade continued to approach slowly. Beneath its pink-lined shelter were his wife, Mrs. Pontellier, and young Robert Lebrun. When they reached the cottage, the two seated themselves with some appearance of fatigue upon the upper step of the porch, facing each other, each leaning against a supporting post.

"What folly! to bathe at such an hour in such heat!" exclaimed Mr. Pontellier. He himself had taken a plunge at daylight. That was why the morning seemed long to him.

"You are burnt beyond recognition," he added, looking at his wife as one looks at a valuable piece of personal property which has suffered some damage.

A paragraph later, and Leonce has wandered off, alone, to Klein's hotel to play a game of billiards. His wife is left alone for the evening to have dinner by herself.

When Leonce returns at eleven o'clock that night, it is he who presumes to be irritated with Edna. Chopin's prose fills with irony:

> He thought it very discouraging that his wife, who was the sole object of his existence, evinced so little interest in things which concerned him, and valued so little his conversation.

Never mind that he manifests no interest in his object, ignores her day and night, and makes no effort to discover the experience of her conversation. Pontellier cannot see the answers to his own questions:

> He reproached his wife with her inattention, her habitual neglect of the children. If it was not a mother's place to look after children, whose on earth was it?

Yes, whose? Having promised his children bonbons and peanuts when he departed to enjoy his billiards, he returns with empty pockets, ready to reproach Edna for her neglect. In his billiardful absence, young Robert Lebrun has played with his children. Though it is early in the novel, Edna's despair in the captivity of this absurd marriage is already acute:

An indescribable oppression, which seemed to generate in some unfamiliar part of her consciousness, filled her whole being with a vague anguish. It was like a shadow, like a mist passing across her soul's summer day.

The next day, Leonce departs for the city for a summer week, leaving his wife a gift of money.

The shadow lengthens. By chapter seventeen, Edna has become alienated not only from Leonce but from society as well. She has become Marginal Woman and has gone out on Tuesday, her normal reception day. When Leonce finds that Edna has not been at home to receive the guests who arrived, he is not worried about her; rather, he is worried about his career:

Mr. Pontellier scanned the names of his wife's callers reading some of them aloud, with comments as he read.

"'The misses Delasidas,' I worked a big deal in futures for their father this morning, nice girls, it's time they were getting married. 'Mrs. Belthrop.' I tell you what it is, Edna; you can't afford to snub Mrs. Belthrop. Why, Belthrop could buy and sell us ten times over. His business is worth a good, round sum to me."

Huffy Leonce, hollow and stuffed, leaves Edna at her dinner table and goes to take his dinner alone at the club.

That night, she takes off her wedding ring, flings it to the floor, and stamps on it.

Like Camus's Mersault in *The Stranger*—an ascetic novel where all colors are white, all relationships are not relationships, and all dialogue expresses meaninglessness—Edna descends into an empty world of alienation, an existential wasteland:

> She felt no interest in anything about her. The street, the children, the fruit vender, the flowers growing there under her eyes, were all part and parcel of an alien world which had suddenly become antagonistic.

When Edna moves out of their home and gets a small place of her own around the corner, Leonce thinks as he is wonted to think:

> ...he begged her to consider first, foremost, and above all else, what people would say. He was not dreaming of scandal when he uttered this warning; that was a thing which would never have entered into his mind to consider in connection with his wife's name or his own. He was simply thinking about his financial integrity...It might do incalculable mischief to his business prospects.

At the beginning of the novel, Edna is enthusiastic about attending her sister's wedding; midway through the pages, she refuses to go. The explanation comes from Leonce's own mouth:

> She won't go to the marriage. She says a wedding is one of the most lamentable spectacles on earth. Nice thing for a woman to say to her husband.

Lamentable spectacle: the first words of the novel, a parrot squawking *Allez vous-en! Allez vous-en! Sapristi!* (Get out! Get out! Damn it!), make more sense all the time. For Edna, her empty marriage is a kind of toxic catalyst; it hastens the chemistry of Edna's disaffection and turns her eyes to the vacancies of her existence. No longer living for her husband or marriage, she must ask herself what she is living for, and the answer is not forthcoming. She loves her children, but she cannot live only for her children. She loves Robert, but she can not live only for Robert, or allow Robert to assume Leonce Pontellier's former role as her owner. When she and Robert are finally alone together, she chides him for not approaching her:

"Why have you been fighting against it?" she asked. Her face glowed with soft lights.

"Why? Because you were not free; you were Leonce Pontellier's wife....Something put into my head that you cared for me, and I lost my senses. I forgot everything but a wild dream of your some way becoming my wife."

"Your wife!"

"Religion, loyalty, everything would give way if only you cared."

"Then you must have forgotten that I was Leonce Pontellier's wife."

"Oh, I was demented, dreaming of wild, impossible things, recalling men who had set their wives free, we have heard of such things."

"Yes, we have heard of such things."

. . .

She took his face between her hands and looked into it as if she would never withdraw her eyes more.

She kissed him on the forehead, the eyes, the cheeks, and the lips.

"You have been a very, very foolish boy, wasting your time dreaming of impossible things when you speak of Mr. Pontellier setting me free! I am no longer one of Mr. Pontellier's possessions to dispose of or not. I give myself where I choose. If he were to say, 'Here, Robert, take her and be happy, she is yours,' I should laugh at you both.

His face grew a little white. "What do you mean?" he asked.

A nice guy, Robert, but far behind Edna. As she later thinks, "He did not know; he did not understand. He would never understand." She has already gone where he can never follow, and even her being there makes him uncomfortable. She has awakened from the illusion of conventional life, and he has not. What do you mean? he gasps, as she scoffs at the idea of being owned, even by him. He leaves her, soon and forever, severing her last human tie.

Throughout the novel, the path of Edna's thought is precarious. Early on, we read: "A certain light was beginning to dawn dimly within her—the light which, showing the way, forbids it."

In short, Mrs. Pontellier was beginning to realize her position in the universe as a human being, and to recognize her relations as an individual to the world within and about her.

Edna is gradually pulled into a Hamlet-like introspection, symbolized by Chopin by the lethal yet alluring voice of the sea:

The voice of the sea is seductive; never ceasing, whispering, clamoring, murmuring, inviting the soul to wander for a spell in abysses of solitude; to lose itself in mazes of inward contemplation.

Edna follows the maze, pursues the track of her inward contemplation, and sinks into the abyss of solitude. Her awakening is freeing, but isolating:

"Yes," she said. "The years that are gone seem like dreams—if one might go on sleeping and dreaming— but to wake up and find—oh! well! perhaps it is better to wake up after all, even to suffer, rather than to remain a dupe to illusions all one's life."

Little by little, the cables that connect her to society and family are disconnected, and in the end she annihilates herself in the sea. Even her new-born love of Robert Lebrun is not enough to save her:

Despondency had come upon her there in the wakeful night, and had never lifted. There was no one thing in the world that she desired. There was no human being whom she wanted near her except Robert; and she even realized that the day would come when he, too, and the thought of him would melt out of her existence, leaving her alone. The children appeared before her like antagonists who had overcome her, who had overpowered and sought to drag her into the soul's slavery for the rest of her days. But she knew a way to elude them. She was not thinking of these things when she walked down to the beach.

A poor swimmer, she walks into the sea and swims

out, farther and farther, until she is too weak to continue. It is over.

We read Edna's last thoughts, close the pages of the book, and put it down. A century ago, Kate Chopin died, dishonored and ostracized. What she had done to earn such obloquy and opprobrium was to write a book that would appeal not solely to future feminists but to everyone who awakens in what Octavio Paz has called the labyrinth of solitude. *The Awakening* is a work of literary art that has no trace of the supermarket novel; rather, its kin are such explorations of the soul as Camus's *The Stranger*, Flaubert's *Madame Bovary*, and even Brontë's *Jane Eyre*. In her lonely labyrinth, Edna Pontellier found walls of tradition, marriage, social expectation, and personal confusion. She did not find an honest path out of the labyrinth, and at length she turned her back on the exits. Her final decision, though it cannot be endorsed, can at least be described: it was her own decision.

What would Kate Chopin think, now, of the world's revised understanding of her work? She would probably be pleased; after all, the option she chose in the face of misunderstanding and disgrace was not the same one Edna Pontellier chose.

It was life.

Absurd, perhaps.

Ironic, surely.

But life.

SEVENTEEN

Long Day's Journey into Night

Eugene O'Neill

Eugene O'Neill has been called the first American playwright of distinction. He has even been called America's Shakespeare. He won a Pulitzer Prize for *Beyond the Horizon* in 1920, another Pulitzer for *Anna Christie* in 1922, and a third Pulitzer for *Strange Interlude* in 1928. He won the Nobel Prize for Literature in 1936 and as of 1998 remains the only American playwright to win it. His plays loom over all reading lists, are included in the Advanced Placement course reading recommendations, and have been routinely banned by those who think that if playwrights do not mention alcohol, children will not drink.

O'Neill is regarded as revolutionary in his effect on American theater, which had previously inhabited the realm of entertainment but which, under O'Neill's post-Strindberg force, became an artistic instrument for exploring humanity's search for meaning in an existence deprived of God (O'Neill was powerfully affected by the writings of Friedrich Neitzsche and often referred to Nietzsche's famous, if misunderstood, dictum: God is dead.) Just as Hemingway and Salinger would later write in ways that Twain made possible, modern playwrights like Williams and Albee would later write in ways that O'Neill made possible through his life-long theatrical explorations of life's tragic dimensions.

O'Neill's masterpiece, which he intended not to be

performed until twenty-five years after his death, is *Long Day's Journey into Night*, a searingly autobiographical rendering of his own early family life. O'Neill dedicated the play to his third wife, Carlotta, who, at their home Tao House, had created the environment he needed in order to work. She later said that no one would ever know how he suffered in writing the play or how terrifying it was to watch him write it; it was a play, she said, that he simply had to write. In his dedication, written in the minute pencil-script he worked in, he said:

> For Carlotta, on our 12th Wedding
> Anniversary
> Dearest: I give you the original script of this play of old sorrow, written in tears and blood. A sadly inappropriate gift, it would seem, for a day celebrating happiness. But you will understand. I mean it as a tribute to your love and tenderness which gave me the faith in love that enabled me to face my dead at last and write this play—write it with deep pity and understanding and forgiveness for all the four haunted Tyrones.

In this play of old sorrow, O'Neill summons a nuclear family of ghosts, like Mozart summoning his father Leopold in Don Giovanni. His father, James O'Neill, an 1880s matinee idol, is now James Tyrone, and the word-play on *tyrant* is not unintentional. His mother is now Mary Tyrone, his brother Jamie is now Jamie Tyrone, and he himself is now Edmund Tyrone.

In the four-act play, the tragedies that afflicted O'Neill's brilliant family are relived in the unsparing truth of fiction; in a seaside summer house surrounded by ever-thickening fog, the dysfunctional family sinks into a foggy oblivion of alcohol (James, Jamie, and Edmund), morphine (Mary), and denial (all). Edmund is diagnosed with consumption, as O'Neill himself had been at the age of twenty-four. Jamie is a brilliant, jaded alcoholic, addicted to prostitutes and failure, as O'Neill's real older brother Jamie had been. And James Tyrone is a self-pitying boozer, a miser, a disappointed former acting talent, and a weary father who denies the insidious effects of his drinking and his penny-pinching on his family.

In Act One, the morning is bright, and the Tyrones seem cheerful, almost normal, at home. We become aware of problems gradually, as the indirections and insinuations make themselves felt through conversation. Apparently, we realize, something is wrong with Edmund:

MARY
   You mustn't mind Edmund, James. Remember he isn't well.
   Edmund can be heard coughing as he goes upstairs. She adds nervously.
   A summer cold makes anyone irritable.

JAMIE
   Genuinely concerned.
   It's not just a cold he's got. The Kid is damned sick.
   His father gives him a sharp warning look but he doesn't see it.

MARY
   Turns on him resentfully.
   Why do you say that? It is just a cold! Anyone can

tell that! You always imagine things.

TYRONE (father)
With another warning glance at Jamie—easily.
All Jamie meant was Edmund might have a touch of something else, too, which makes his cold worse.

JAMIE
Sure, Mama. That's all I meant.

It is not all he meant, and what Edmund has a touch of is tuberculosis. Throughout the play, Mary denies Edmund's consumption, calling the doctor a quack, calling the cough a cold, becoming angry whenever anyone tells her the truth, and retreating into a gray fog of morphine as a defense against the pain. Even in Act Four, she has not accepted the truth; when Edmund interrupts her in frustration over her denial, her reaction is immediate, even through her morphine stupor:

EDMUND
Turns impulsively and grabs her arm. As he pleads he has the quality of a bewilderingly hurt little boy.
Mama! It isn't a summer cold! I've got consumption.

MARY
For a second he seems to have broken through to her. She trembles and her expression becomes terrified. She calls distractedly, as if giving a command to herself.
No!
And instantly she is far away again.

And Edmund's illness is not all that is wrong. The first words of the play, Tyrone's "You're a fine armful now, Mary, with those twenty pounds you've gained," are soon understood as a reference to Mary's morphine addiction, which she acquired as a result of medical treatment associated with a difficult birth. She has just returned from a sanatorium, has gained some health and weight back, and her husband and sons are filled with fearful hope that she will finally kick her habit. It is a touchy subject, one just beneath the surface of decorum:

MARY

Of course, there's nothing takes away your appetite like a bad summer cold.

TYRONE

Yes, it's only natural. So don't let yourself get worried—

MARY

Quickly.

Oh, I'm not. I know he'll be all right in a few days if he takes care of himself.

As if she wanted to dismiss the subject but can't.

But it does seem a shame he should have to be sick right now.

TYRONE

Yes, it is bad luck.

He gives her a quick, worried look.

But you mustn't let it upset you, Mary. Remember, you've got to take care of yourself, too.

MARY
    Quickly.
    I'm not upset. There's nothing to be upset about.
What makes you think I'm upset?

The lady doth protest too much. She is upset, and she
is not taking care of herself. On the contrary. She has
already begun sneaking off alone, getting her fix.
    And then resentments begin boiling to the surface.
First, Jamie attacks James for miserliness, blaming
Edmund's consumption on lack of proper medical
treatment:

JAMIE
    He turns on his father accusingly.
    It might never have happened if you'd sent him to
a real doctor when he first got sick.

TYRONE
    What's the matter with Hardy? He's always been
our doctor up here.

JAMIE
    Everything's the matter with him. Even in this hick
burg he's rated third class! He's a cheap old quack!

TYRONE
    That's right! Run him down! Run down everybody!
Everyone is a fake to you!

JAMIE
Contemptuously.
    Hardy only charges a dollar. That's what makes
you think he's a fine doctor!

Wounded and defensive, Tyrone has some scores of his own to settle:

TYRONE
Accusingly.
The less you say about Edmund's sickness, the better for your conscience! You're more responsible than anyone!

JAMIE
Stung.
That's a lie! I won't stand for that, Papa!

TYRONE
It's the truth. You've been the worst influence for him. He grew up admiring you as a hero! A fine example you set him! If you ever gave him advice except in the ways of rottenness, I've never heard of it! You made him old before his time, pumping him full of what you consider worldly wisdom, when he was too young to see that your mind was poisoned by your own failure in life, you wanted to believe every man was a knave with his soul for sale, and every woman who wasn't a whore was a fool!

These are hard words, hard father-son words. We begin to understand Carlotta O'Neill's description of O'Neill at work on this play: terrifying, she said. And we begin to understand, even in Act One, why O'Neill referred to the great triumvirate—pity, understanding, and forgiveness—in his dedication. By the end of Act One, we learn that Jamie has heard his mother moving about late at night in ways reminiscent of her former addictive habits; he begs her to take care of herself, she responds with unconvincing denial, and as Act One ends, she is going upstairs alone to "take a nap." A narcotic nap, we somehow know.

And the drinking has not even begun.

In Act Two, the fog thickens with the plot. The day is now described as sultry with a faint haziness. In this haziness, the boys (young adults, thirty-three and twenty-three) begin drinking, stealing their father's whiskey while he is outside working on the hedge, and adding water to the bottle so that he will not know they have taken it. The alcohol begins to take effect, and Jamie begins sneering at his father, incurring his mother's ire; suddenly she drifts into a detached, impersonal tone that discloses, for a moment, both her own humanity and Eugene O'Neill's forgiveness:

MARY
    Bitterly.
Because he's always sneering at someone else, always looking for the worst weakness in everyone.
    Then, with a strange, abrupt change to a . . . . detached, impersonal tone.

But I suppose life has made him like that, and he can't help it. None of us can help the things life has done to us. They're done before you realize it, and once they're done they make you do other things until at last everything comes between you and what you'd like to be, and you've lost your true self forever.

No one in this family, we see more and more deeply, is what they'd like to be. They have all lost their true selves forever, and yet they all know and love the lost selves they see in each and other and in themselves. By the end of Act Two, Scene One, Jamie and even James have confronted Mary directly about her return to morphine (she does not know what they mean), James is drinking with his sons, and the family sits down to lunch. In Scene Two, the pleasant dispositions have hardened into shells of guilt and blame, the doctor calls to make an appointment informing the Tyrones that Edmund has tuberculosis, and Mary has ridden demon morphine into a garrulous obtuseness, which her husband and sons recognize as a narcotic fog that will only thicken as the long day journeys into night. Talking to Edmund, Mary suddenly achieves a moment of lucid introspection:

> How could you believe me—when I can't believe myself? I've become such a liar. I never lied about anything once upon a time. Now I have to lie, especially to myself. But how can you understand, when I don't myself. I've never understood anything about it, except that one day long ago I found I could no longer call my soul my own.

Act Three.
Night is coming.
The fog rolls in.
Mary says that she loves the fog: "It hides you from the world and the world from you. You feel that everything has changed, and nothing is what it seemed to be. No one can find or touch you any more." And minutes later: "How thick the fog is. I can't see the road. All the people in the world could pass by and I would never know. I wish it was always that way. It's getting dark already. It will soon be night, thank goodness."

It will soon be night, externally and internally. Mary

talks discursively to her servant, Cathleen, the foghorn sounds its gloomy warning through the dimness, and Mary tries to "find the faith I lost, so I could pray again!" She pauses, and tries to say her Hail Mary, but like Hamlet's uncle-father, Claudius, she cannot pray:

> "Hail Mary, full of grace! The Lord is with Thee; blessed art Thou among women."
> *Sneeringly.*
> You expect the Blessed Virgin to be fooled by a lying dope fiend reciting words! You can't hide from her!
> *She springs to her feet. Her hands fly up to pat her hair distractedly.*
> I must go upstairs. I haven't taken enough. When you start again you never know exactly how much you need.

With her hands, her words fly up; her thoughts remain below, and words without thoughts never to Heaven go. The act ends in a crescendo of interactions; James comes home and they state their love for each other, but Mary drifts off into pathetic memories of being left alone in cheap hotels while her husband spent his evenings in bars; Edmund returns from the doctor visit and tries to tell his mother that he does have consumption and will have to go to a sanatorium, but Mary falls into a slough of denial, blaming Doc Hardy's lies. The act ends miserably with Edmund calling his mother a "dope fiend" and her slinking upstairs, as Tyrone calls after her about the poison she is going to take.

Act Four.

Midnight.

Dense wall of fog.

Lights out.

Edmund and Tyrone share the living room, drinking and discussing the fog. Edmund sounds more and more like his mother. He says, "The fog was where I wanted to be...I didn't meet a soul. Everything looked and sounded unreal. Nothing was what it is. That's what I wanted—to be alone with myself in another world where truth is untrue and lie can hide from itself."

They drink.

They play cards.

They drink.

They try to discuss Mary's problems:

EDMUND

Yes. It's pretty horrible to see her the way she must be now.

With bitter misery.

The hardest thing to take is the blank wall she builds around her. Or it's more like a bank of fog in which she hides and loses herself.

Edmund sinks into recrimination, blaming his father's miserliness for Mary's addiction; if James would have paid for a proper doctor, a quack would never have put her on morphine, and if James would have immediately sent her to a proper treatment center, she could have been cured while there was still time. "You lie," Tyrone, shouts, but he has been wounded. From there, they move to a discussion about Edmund's own situation and the cost of sending him to a private sanatorium, rather than the cheap state sanatorium that James intends. Eventually, James ambivalently submits:

You have to look for bargains. If I took this state farm sanatorium for a good bargain, you'll have to forgive me. The doctors did tell me it's a good place. You must believe that, Edmund. And I swear I never meant you to go there if you didn't want to.

Vehemently.

You can choose any place you like! Never mind what it costs! Any place I can afford. Any place you like—within reason.

He then steers Edmund toward another cheap place: "It's only seven dollars a week but you get ten times that value."

They play cards, but the authenticity of their exchange—and the seriousness of his son's illness—has moved Tyrone, and he begins to tell Edmund of his early acting career, when he showed an extraordinary talent. Having a gift for Shakespeare, he sank into the easy and lucrative life of a box office success and never fulfilled his potential. And now, he feels, "I'd be willing to have no home but the poorhouse in my old age if I could look back now on having been the fine artist I might have been."

Confession breeds confession, and Edmund tells his father about his years at sea, when he sometimes felt himself merging with the elements:

I lay on the bowsprit, facing astern, with the water foaming into spume under me, the masts with every sail white in the moonlight, towering high above me. I became drunk with the beauty and singing rhythm of it, and for a moment I lost myself—actually lost my life. I was set free! I dissolved in the sea, became white sails and flying spray, became beauty and rhythm, became moonlight and the ship and the high dim-starred sky! I belonged....For a second there is meaning! Then the hand lets the veil fall and you are alone, lost in the fog again, and you stumble on toward nowhere, for no good reason!

He grins wryly.

It was a great mistake, my being born a man, I would have been much more successful as a sea gull or a fish.

When James hears these words and tells Edmund that he has the makings of a poet, Edmund demurs, and we see the inner workings of O'Neill's mind:

The makings of a poet. No, I'm afraid I'm like the guy who is always panhandling for a smoke. He hasn't even got the makings. He's got only the habit. I couldn't touch what I tried to tell you just now. I just stammered. That's the best I'll ever do, I mean, if I live. Well, it will be faithful realism, at least. Stammering is the native eloquence of us fog people.

Us fog people—enter elder brother Jamie, fresh from an alcoholic binge and a house of ill repute. James cannot take it and leaves the room for the safety of the porch. Slurring his words, Jamie accosts Edmund with tales of his adventures, referring to James as "old Gaspard" and describing his evening with Fat Violet, his lady of the night. Eventually, Jamie lurches into a *vino veritas* confession of his ambivalence toward Edmund and warns him against himself:

I've been rotten bad influence. And worst of it is, I did it on purpose....You listen! Did it on purpose to make a bum of you. Or part of me did. A big part. That part that's been dead so long. That hates life....Made my mistakes look good. Made getting drunk romantic. Made whores fascinating vampires instead of poor, stupid, diseased slobs they really are. Made fun of work as a sucker's game. Never wanted you succeed and make me look even worse by comparison. Wanted you to fail. Always jealous of you. Mama's baby, Papa's pet!

Telling Edmund he loves him more than he hates him, Jamie asks Edmund to think of him as dead and falls into a drunken sleep. Tyrone creeps back in, but Jamie wakes up and begins quoting Rosetti: "Look in my face. My name is Might-Have-Been." Tempers flame up, Jamie falls into drunken sleep again, but suddenly the lights come on: pathetic, Mary is pitifully holding her wedding gown; James and Edmund gape, and Jamie wakes again: "The Mad Scene," he cries, "Enter Ophelia!"

It is beyond horrible.

Edmund strikes Jamie in the face, and Tyrone says he'll kick him out into the gutter tomorrow, but Mary begins to speak, and all three men are struck into silence. It is too like the Mad Scene; we wait for the words "How do you pretty lady," but Mary enters, and James moves to take her wedding gown. Like Ophelia, Mary is only partly aware of her surroundings; much of her mind is absorbed in private pain that she partially voices, and she keeps saying she is looking for something that she has lost, something that she misses terribly, something she needs terribly. When she had it she was never lonely or afraid. The pain of the scene is excruciating.

It is here where Edmund cries "I have consumption," and she screams back "NO," and the play ends with her remembering her days in the convent, when Mother Elizabeth would understand her. But Mother Elizabeth had asked Mary to be sure about her faith and to test it by leaving the convent until she was sure:

> That was in the winter of senior year. Then in the spring something happened to me. Yes, I remember. I fell in love with James Tyrone and was so happy for a time.

> She stares before her in a sad dream. Tyrone stirs in his chair. Edmund and Jamie remain motionless.

CURTAIN

It is over. I was so happy for a time. For a time. As members of O'Neill's audience, we are exhausted and heartbroken, trapped between revulsion for this cruel and self-destructive family and an absolutely profound empathy we did not know we were capable of.

We leave the theater, or the book, needing time to compose our feelings, never mind our thoughts.

But later, when we have done that, understanding begins to emerge. And pity. And forgiveness. The triumvirate.

Perhaps today the dysfunction of this family would be called codependent—a foolish figure, and farewell it, for we will use no pop psychology. Yes, the relationships displayed here are not happy ones, and the lives are not productive, but with every reading of *Long Day's Journey into Night*, we become more aware of the goodness amid the tragedy.

We become struck by the Tyrone family's staying. They stay. No matter how bad it gets, no matter how severe the blame, the guilt, the regret, no matter how painful the sight of drunken father or narcotized mother, of consumptive son or dissolute brother, they stay. It seems not to occur to any of them that they could leave. Go somewhere else. Start life over. No, this is life. This family. For all of their horrors, they are a family, and it is to each other that they return, loving and hating, apologizing and abusing.

Apologizing—there is another constant in their behavior. Almost as frequent as their acrimony is their regret; they constantly apologize to each other. Instantly after hurting Edmund's feelings, Jamie is saying, "I'm sorry kid, I didn't mean that." And they all do it. They cannot stop saying the terrible things, for foul pains will rise though all the earth o'erwhelm them, but having said them, they are sorry; it hurts them to hurt each other.

For in the end, they love each other.

Pity, understanding, and forgiveness. The end result of Eugene O'Neill's piercing self-disclosure is that we, as he must have, feel these necessary things. For all of their failure, weakness, and wrongdoing, the Tyrones still move us and capture our regard; they are not worthless to us; we do not turn from them, discard them, or even much condemn them.

Somehow, we suffer with them; somehow, their essential humanity survives; their nightmare is not entirely of their own making, and their agony is somehow worse because they care. If any of the Tyrones were coldly egocentric, brutal, or indifferent to the hearts of the others, we would condemn them, but they are not, and we do not. Mary told James: "And I love you, dear, in spite of everything." Through the words of this play, Eugene O'Neill was saying the same thing to his family and to himself.

EIGHTEEN

The Demon-Haunted World

Carl Sagan

In the preface to his final book *The Demon-Haunted World*, Carl Sagan, professor of astronomy at Cornell University and the author of *Cosmos*, the best-selling science book of all time, described his early education:

I wish I could tell you about inspirational teachers in science from my elementary or junior high or high school days. But as I think back on it, there were none. There was rote memorization about the Periodic Table of the Elements, levers and inclined planes, green plant photosynthesis, and the difference between anthracite and bituminous coal. But there was no soaring sense of wonder, no hint of an evolutionary perspective, and nothing about mistaken ideas that everybody had once believed. In high school laboratory courses, there was an answer we were supposed to get. We were marked off if we didn't get it. There was no encouragement to pursue our own interests or hunches or conceptual mistakes. In the backs of textbooks there was material you could tell was interesting. The school year would always end before we got to it. You could find wonderful books on astronomy, say, in the libraries, but not in the classroom. Long division was taught as a set of rules from a cookbook, with no explanation of how this particular sequence of short divisions, multiplications, and subtractions got you the right answer. In high school, extracting square roots was offered reverentially, as if it were a method once handed down from Mt. Sinai. It was our job merely to remember what we had been commanded. Get the right answer, and never mind that you don't understand what you're doing.

With that, Sagan begins his journey through the tortured landscape of pseudoscience, encountering along the way such demons as the supposed face on Mars, flying saucers, alien abductions, witchcraft, divine visitations, and crop circles. The book has been described as a polemic by those who would resist the quality of its argument, but in fact it is much more than a polemic by a controversialist; it is an extended discussion by one of the world's leading—and most humane—scientists of the plague of x-flies that infest our popular culture. In *The Demon-Haunted World*, Carl Sagan patiently and lucidly explains the nature, purpose, and method of real science and distinguishes it from the false nature, mispurpose, and mercenary deception of pseudoscience. With striking respect for les miserables who believe in the faux phenomena of pseudoscience—such as those who sincerely believe they have been abducted by aliens—Sagan delineates the essential facts of these myths, always stressing that science, in stark contrast with pseudoscience, is a method designed to find the real truth, never mind how the truth makes anyone feel. Science has, Sagan insists, a "stuffy skeptical rigor." It is the understanding of this rigor, this superb investigative method, that is missing in the public mind. And why, Sagan asks, should the public understand? Neither in our schools nor in our mass media do we teach science as a method; we only teach science as a set of findings. And yet:

> If we teach only the findings and products of science—no matter how useful and even inspiring they may be—without communicating its critical method, how can the average person possibly distinguish science from pseudoscience? Both then are presented as unsupported assertion.

In fact, Sagan argues, "The method of science, as stodgy and grumpy as it may seem, is far more important than the findings of science." This grumpy method has produced innumerable benefits for humanity, including the medical knowledge that is responsible for most of us being alive. And as this knowledge increases, our dependence on science increases; we are, Sagan says, stuck with science. But superstition and pseudoscience keep getting in the way, distracting the credulous:

> ... providing easy answers, dodging skeptical scrutiny, casually pressing our awe buttons and cheapening the experience, making us routine and comfortable practitioners as well as victims of credulity. Yes, the world would be a more interesting place if there were UFOs lurking in the deep waters off Bermuda and eating ships and planes, or if dead people could take control of our hands and write us messages . . .

These are all instances of pseudoscience. They purport to use the methods and findings of science, while in fact they are faithless to its nature—often because they are based on insufficient evidence or because they ignore clues that point the other way. They ripple with gullibility.

One of Sagan's most interesting distinctions is that pseudoscience is not merely erroneous science. Indeed, it is not even erroneous science:

> Pseudoscience differs from erroneous science. Science thrives on errors, cutting them away one by one. False conclusions are drawn all the time, but they are drawn tentatively. Hypotheses are framed so they are capable of being disproved. A succession of alternative hypotheses is confronted by experiment and observation. Science gropes and staggers toward improved understanding. Proprietary feelings are of course offended when a scientific hypothesis is disproved, but such disproofs are recognized as central to the scientific enterprise.

Scientists, Sagan shows, reject mystic revelations for which there is no evidence except somebody's say-so; pseudoscience devotees regard somebody's say-so as evidence. The distinction is critical.

But what if the somebody is an authority? A specialist? No. In science, somebody's say-so is not evidence; the evidence is an independent experimental confirmation that anybody's say-so is true.

> One of the great commandments of science is, "Mistrust arguments from authority."...Too many such arguments have proved too painfully wrong. Authorities must prove their contentions like everybody else. This independence of science, its occasional unwillingness to accept conventional wisdom, makes it dangerous to doctrines less self-critical, or with pretensions to certitude.

Authorities must prove their contentions like everybody else. Talk about a level playing field. "It makes no difference," Sagan says, "how smart, august, or beloved you are. You must prove your case in the face of determined, expert criticism." Scientists publish their findings in refereed journals, allowing other scientists all over the world to reproduce their experiments, check their calculations, suggest superior explanations of data, and look for errors of all kinds. It is a formidable, intimidating process, but one that is superb for getting at the truth, and for this reason, Sagan says, science "delivers the goods."

> You can go to the witch doctor to lift the spell that causes your pernicious anemia, or you can take vitamin B12. If you want to save your child from polio, you can pray or you can inoculate. If you're interested in the sex of your unborn child, you can consult plumb-bob danglers all you want (left-right, a boy; forward-back, a girl—or maybe it's the other way around), but they'll be right, on average, only one time in two. If you want real accuracy (here, 99 percent accuracy), try amniocentesis and sonograms. Try science.

At this, plumb-bob danglers might be offended, but to the scientific method, this is irrelevant. "There are no forbidden questions in science, no matters too sensitive or delicate to be probed, no sacred truths. That openness to new ideas, combined with the most rigorous, skeptical scrutiny of all ideas, sifts the wheat from the chaff."

And what wheat survives this method of intense skeptical scrutiny? Newton's laws of motion and the inverse square law of gravitation:

Years after launch, billions of miles from Earth (with only tiny corrections from Einstein), the spacecraft beautifully arrives at a predetermined point in the orbit of the target world, just as the world comes ambling by. The accuracy is astonishing. Plainly, Newton knew what he was doing.

Having focused our comprehensions on the exact nature of the scientific method, Sagan turns that method on the stars of pseudoscience, the pop demons of the demon-haunted world.

Such as?

Such as the face on Mars. Sagan reviews similar misimpressions: that there was a man in the Moon, that there were canals visible on Mars. "Hundreds of canals were mapped and named," Sagan writes, "But, oddly, they avoided showing up on photographs." As for the face:

Mars has a surface area of almost 150 million square kilometers, about the land area of the earth. The area covered by the Martian "sphinx" is about one square kilometer. Is it so astonishing that one (comparatively) postage-stamp-sized patch in 150 million should look artificial—especially given our penchant, since infancy, for finding faces? When we examine the neighboring jumble of hillocks, mesas, and other complex surface forms, we recognize that the feature is akin to many that do not at all resemble a human face. Why this resemblance? Would the ancient Martian engineers rework only this mesa (well, maybe a few others) and leave all others unimproved by monumental sculpture? Or shall we conclude that other blocky mesas are also sculpted into the form of faces, but weirder faces, unfamiliar to us on Earth?

If we study the original image more carefully, we find that a strategically placed "nostril"—one that adds much to the impression of a face— is in fact a black dot corresponding to lost data in the radio transmission from Mars to Earth.

And as for alien abductions and alien experiments on human beings, including alien breeding programs using human beings as guinea pigs (Do not laugh; Sagan reminds us that polls show most Americans believe that the Earth is being visited by aliens in UFOs and that more than three million Americans believe they have been abducted by aliens), Sagan has a few questions about the details that often are reported:

Why should beings so advanced in physics and engineering—crossing vast interstellar distances, walking like ghosts through walls—be so backward when it comes to biology? Why, if the aliens are trying to do their business in secret, wouldn't they perfectly expunge all memories of the abductions? Too hard for them to do? Why are all the examining instruments macroscopic and so reminiscent of what can be found at the neighborhood medical clinic? Why go to all the trouble of repeated sexual encounters between aliens and humans? Why not steal a few egg and sperm cells, read the full genetic code, and then manufacture as many copies as you like with whatever genetic variations happen to suit your fancy? Even we humans, who as yet cannot quickly cross interstellar space or slither through walls, are able to clone cells. How could humans be the result of an alien breeding program if we share 99.6 percent of our active genes with the chimpanzees? We're more closely related to chimpanzees than rats are to mice.

Remember, this skepticism comes from perhaps the most respect pro-alien scientist in the word, a scientist who championed the SETI project and who believed profoundly that the universe teems with life. Sagan explains:

> I had been interested in the possibility of extraterrestrial life from childhood, from long before I ever heard of flying saucers. I've remained fascinated long after my early enthusiasm for UFOs waned—as I understood more about that remorseless taskmaster called the scientific method: Everything hinges on the matter of evidence. On so important a question [as alien visitation], the evidence must be airtight. The more we want it to be true, the more careful we have to be. No witness's say-so is good enough. People make mistakes. People play practical jokes. People stretch the truth for money or attention or fame. People occasionally misunderstand what they are seeing. People sometimes even see things that aren't there.

Sagan points out that even the name *flying saucer* is a mistake, based on the press's misunderstanding of pilot Kenneth Arnold's description of lights that moved like saucers skipping on water; Arnold never said that they were shaped like saucers.

Sagan reviews the stories: alien wreckage that turned out to be made of kitchen-pot aluminum, and alien crop circles that turned out to be made by Doug and Dave:

> In 1991, Doug Bower and Dave Chorley, two blokes from Southhampton, announced they had been making crop figures for 15 years. They dreamed it up over stout one evening in their regular pub, The Percy Hobbes. They had been amused by UFO reports and thought it might be fun to spoof the UFO gullibles. At first they flattened the wheat with the heavy steel bar that Bower used as a security device on the back door of his picture framing shop. Later on they used planks and ropes. Their first efforts took only a few minutes.But, being inveterate pranksters as well as serious artists, the challenge began to grow on them. Gradually, they designed and executed more and more demanding figures.

At first, no one noticed Doug and Dave's crop circles. Just when they were about to cease in disappointment, the things caught on, and the alien crop circle craze began. Soon copycat circlers began making their own circles in Britain and Europe. In time, Doug and Dave wearied of their prank and confessed (Read *Round in Circles*; Penguin Books, 1994), but the confession was not headline news, and many cerealogists (ha ha ha ha) refused to believe the confession! Sagan laments: "Our politics, economics, advertising, and religions (New Age and Old) are awash in credulity."

Credulity. In a chapter entitled "The Fine Art of Baloney Detection," Sagan considers "channelers" who claim to achieve communication with the dead. Communication with the dead, Sagan agrees, is a power devoutly to be wished; he longs to communicate with his own parents. But this does not mean, he insists, that he wishes to fall victim to a hoax. His questions are devastating:

> How is it, I ask myself, that channelers never give us verifiable information otherwise unavailable?

Consider that question carefully before we go on:

> How is it, I ask myself, that channelers never give us verifiable information otherwise unavailable? Why does Alexander the Great never tell us about the exact location of his tomb, Fermat about his Last Theorem, John Wilkes Booth about the Lincoln assassination conspiracy, Hermann Göring about the Reichstag fire? Why don't Sophocles, Democritus, and Aristarchus dictate their lost books? Don't they wish future generations to have access to their masterpieces?

The answer, of course, is that channelers are charlatans who know no verifiable information, from the dead or otherwise. We have never received news from the dead.

In this Baloney Detection chapter, Sagan lists and explains a number of Tools for Skeptical Thinking. These include independent confirmation, substantive debate, the rejection of argument from authority, the consideration of multiple hypotheses, the avoidance of attachment to a hypothesis, quantification, the insistence that every link in an argument chain hold up, Occam's Razor, and careful avoidance of numerous logical fallacies, including the misunderstanding of statistics:

...misunderstanding of the nature of statistics (e.g., President Dwight Eisenhower expressing astonishment and alarm on discovering that fully half of all Americans have below average intelligence).

Sometimes, Sagan's incredulity rises to a level that must seize our attention:

> When the first work was published in the scientific literature in 1953 showing that the substances in cigarette smoke when painted on the backs of rodents produced malignancies, the response of the six major tobacco companies was to initiate a public relations campaign to impugn the research, sponsored by the Sloan Kettering Foundation. This is similar to what the Du Pont Corporation did when the first research was published in 1974 showing that their Freon product attacks the protective ozone layer. There are many other examples.
>
> You might think that before they denounce unwelcome research findings, major corporations would devote their considerable resources to checking out the safety of the products they propose to manufacture. And if they missed something, if independent scientists suggest a hazard, why would the companies protest? Would they rather kill people than lose profits?

He is equally incredulous over the widespread belief in astrology. A quarter of all Americans believe in astrology. A third think that sun-sign astrology is "scientific." The percentage of schoolchildren who believe in astrology rose from forty percent in 1978 to fifty-nine percent in 1984. In the United States, there are ten times more astrologers than astronomers. No matter that astrology is demonstrably fatuous:

Many valid criticisms of astrology can be formulated in a few sentences: for example, its acceptance of precession of the equinoxes in announcing an "Age of Aquarius" and its rejection of precession of the equinoxes in casting horoscopes; its neglect of atmospheric refraction; its list of supposedly significant celestial objects that is mainly limited to naked eye objects known to Ptolemy in the second century, and that ignores an enormous variety of new astronomical objects discovered since (where is the astrology of near-Earth asteroids?); inconsistent requirements for detailed information on the time as compared to the latitude and longitude of birth; the failure of astrology to pass the identical-twin test; the major differences in horoscopes cast from the same birth information by different astrologers; and the absence of demonstrated correlation between horoscopes and such psychological tests as the Minnesota Multiphasic Personality Inventory.

At the end of his book, Sagan connects his theme of skeptical scientific method to the failure of American education. Explaining that he sometimes teaches a kindergarten class, he describes little kids as natural-born scientists who are curious and intellectually vigorous, who ask provocative and insightful questions, who exhibit enthusiasm, and who ask follow-up questions. These kids, Sagan explains, have never heard of "dumb questions." But...

But when I talk to high school seniors, I find something different. They memorize "facts." By and large, though, the joy of discovery, the life behind those facts, has gone out of them. They've lost much of the wonder, and gained very little skepticism. They're worried about asking "dumb" questions; they're willing to accept inadequate answers; they don't pose follow-up questions; the room is awash with sidelong glances to judge, second-by-second, the approval of their peers. They come to class with their questions written out on pieces of paper, which they surreptitiously examine, waiting their turn and oblivious of whatever discussion their peers are at this moment engaged in.

Then, in a flurry of pages, Sagan delineates the scope of America's educational disaster:

"It's Official," reads one newspaper headline: "We Stink in Science." In tests of average 17-year-olds in many world regions, the U.S. ranked dead last in algebra. On identical tests, the U.S. kids averaged 43% and their Japanese counterparts 78%. In my book, 78% is pretty good—it corresponds to a C+, or maybe even a B-; 43% is an F. In a chemistry test, students in only two of 13 nations did worse than the U.S. Britain, Singapore, and Hong Kong were so high they were almost off-scale, and 25% of Canadian 18-year-olds knew just as much chemistry as a select 1% of American high school seniors (in their second chemistry course, and most of them in "advanced" placement programs). The best of 20 fifth-grade classrooms in Minneapolis was outpaced by every one of 20 classrooms in Sendai, Japan, and

19 out of 20 in Taipei, Taiwan. South Korean students were far ahead of American students in all aspects of mathematics and science, and 13-year-olds in British Columbia (in Western Canada) outpaced their U.S. counterparts across the board (in some areas they did better than the Koreans). Of the U.S. kids, 22% say they dislike school; only 8% of the Koreans do. Yet two-thirds of the Americans, but only a quarter of the Koreans, say they are "good at mathematics."

Sagan shows that a failing American educational system produces ignorant high school students who become ignorant adults:

Sixty-three percent of American adults are unaware that the last dinosaur died before the first human arose; 75 percent do not know that antibiotics kill bacteria but not viruses; 57 percent do not know that "electrons are smaller than atoms." Polls show that something like half of American adults do not know that the Earth goes around the Sun and takes a year to do it. I can find in my undergraduate classes at Cornell University bright students who do not know that the stars rise and set at night, or even that the Sun is a star.

Well, Sagan asks, what do we expect? "During four years of high school, American students spend less than 1,500 hours on such subjects as mathematics, science, and history. Japanese, French, and German students spend more than twice as much time."

When Sagan's discussion of American education appeared in *Parade* magazine, he received many letters from American students in response. Here are some of the letters Sagan received from tenth graders, with spelling, grammar, and punctuation as in the original letters:

• Not a Americans are stupid We just rank lower in school big deal.
• Maybe that's good that we are not as smart as the other countries. So then we can just import all of our products and then we don't have to spend all of our money on the parts for the goods.
• And if other countries are doing better, what does it matter, their most likely going to come over the U.S. anyway?

Read it and weep, goes the saying.

Carl Sagan's *The Demon-Haunted World* is a lucid and haunting testament, a final plea by one of the world's leading scientists who viewed scientific skepticism as a "candle in the dark." Sagan's enlightened advocacy for the scientific method as an antidote to the vulgar credulity that typifies American popular culture, resulting in a fooling commerce and a fooled public, is something that everyone who loves authentic education should read.

In conclusion? Perhaps the best conclusion to this review is to return to Sagan's own words:

You can go to the witch doctor to lift the spell that causes your pernicious anemia, or you can take vitamin B12. If you want to save your child from polio, you can pray or you can inoculate. If you're interested in the sex of your unborn child, you can consult plumb-bob danglers all you want...but they'll be right, on average, only one time in two. If you want real accuracy (here, 99 percent accuracy), try amniocentesis and sonograms. Try science.

Try science. And in the process, try this book, *The Demon-Haunted World*, which is filled with light and purpose. It is essential reading and will cure the siren symptoms of astrology, telepathy, crop circles, Martian faces, Bermuda triangles, and witchcraft that inflame your organs of clarity.

NINETEEN

The Bell Jar

Sylvia Plath

In W.H. Auden's poetic eulogy of William Butler Yeats, "In Memory of W.B. Yeats," he wrote that now, Yeats was scattered among a hundred cities:

Now he is scattered among a hundred cities
And wholly given over to unfamiliar affections;
To find his happiness in another kind of wood
And be punished under a foreign code of conscience.
The words of a dead man
Are modified in the guts of the living.

Yes, it is a curious thing, in some ways tragic and in other ways fortunate, that the publication of ideas involves their dispersal to other minds, who inevitably reinterpret and reform the ideas, often leaving them, in Yeats's words, changed utterly. And once an author is dead, he or she cannot even say, "No, that is not what I meant at all. That is not it, at all."

Something of this is what we feel in searching the Internet for the term SYLVIA PLATH. There are the expected biographical notes and announcements of new editions of her novel and poems. There are discussions of her relationship with rival poet Anne Sexton. There are serious scholarly exegeses by serious scholarly exegetes. But these are outnumbered by swarming displays of puerile narcissism: Janie's homepage of Poets I Admire,

Bob's My Favorite Stuff, Linda's Home Page, so-and-so's homepage of Some of My Favorite Poets, and someone's homepage of Some of My Favorite Books. To these, we are directed by a search for SYLVIA PLATH. There is even a homepage called, "Some Writers Who Blow Me Away." And there is Sylvia Plath.

In these home pages, we notice the key words:

I.

Me.

My.

Stuff.

My stuff.

How would Sylvia Plath feel, to be omnipresent in the computers of the world as someone's favorite-stuff-that-blows-me-away? Would she feel, as some tribal peoples once felt about photographs, that these documents had stolen her soul?

On the Cosmic Baseball Association homepage, Plath is listed as Pitcher among a team of Vestal Virgins, and the text includes this sentence: "Locating the exact location of fracture in the poet Sylvia Plath's personality has occupied a fair amount of time by the literary-academic-psychoanalytic squads of the cultural elite."

Horrible, horrible, most horrible. The sentence reminds us of Polonius's dumb introduction of "The Mousetrap" within *Hamlet*: comical-tragical, comical-historical-tragical, comical-tragical-historical-pastoral.

We cannot think that Plath would want such alien sentences—with their needless words, incondite structures, and thick fingers—probing the remains of her spirit.

But it cannot be helped. Our concern for the life and ideas of Sylvia Plath continues to increase, and now that the twenty-fifth anniversary of the publication of *The Bell*

Jar has arrived, our interest in her novel has discovered a concomitant renaissance. And perhaps we can even forgive the host of golden home page authors who are guilty of youthful egocentrism, and whose sensitivities are still emergent.

Our concern for Sylvia Plath continues to increase.

Sylvia Plath was born in 1932 in Jamaica Plain, Massachusetts. Her father died when she was eight. A straight-A student, Sylvia went to Smith College on scholarship. At Smith, she wrote over four hundred poems. In the summer after her junior year at Smith, Sylvia went to New York as a guest editor of *Mademoiselle* magazine. Returning home from New York, she attempted suicide with sleeping pills and nearly succeeded. The subsequent therapy included electroshock. She later remembered this experience in *The Bell Jar*, which now has sold more than two million copies in the United States. In 1956 Plath married English poet and future Poet Laureate Ted Hughes. After their marriage failed, Sylvia committed suicide with the gas from a cook stove, leaving two children. She was thirty. *Ariel*, a brilliant collection of her last poems, was published posthumously in 1965. In the years since her death, her life and work have been the subject of numerous memoirs, analyses, and biographies, and she has attained major influence status, both as a brilliant poet and as a forceful early feminist.

A bell jar is a bell-shaped glass jar that is used either to cover and protect something displayed, such as an instrument, or to isolate its interior atmosphere from the exterior, separating a gas or a vacuum from the environment.

In *The Bell Jar*, Plath described the stifling air of her alter ego Esther Greenwood's personality:

I knew I should be grateful to Mrs. Guinea, only I couldn't feel a thing. If Mrs. Guinea had given me a ticket to Europe, or a round-the-world cruise, it wouldn't have made one scrap of difference to me, because wherever I sat—on the deck of a ship or at a street café in Paris or Bangkok—I would be sitting under the same glass bell jar, stewing in my own sour air.

After her second electroshock treatment, Esther wakes from a deep sleep:

All the heat and fear purged itself. I felt surprisingly at peace. The bell jar hung, suspended, a few feet above my head. I was open to the circulating air.

When Esther is released from the hospital, she drives home with her mother. Her mother tries to say something encouraging:

"We'll take up where we left off, Esther," she had said, with her sweet, martyr's smile. "We'll act as if all this were a bad dream."
A bad dream.
To the person in the bell jar, blank and stopped as a dead baby, the world itself is a bad dream.

In the end, though proclaimed recovered, Esther is filled with pensive introspection:

How did I know that someday—at college, in Europe, somewhere, anywhere—the bell jar, with its stifling distortions, wouldn't descend again?

The bell jar did descend again over Sylvia Plath's spirit, leaving her blank and stopped as a dead baby, cutting her off from the circulating air and leaving her stewing in her own sour air. And now she is scattered among a hundred homepages, being punished under a foreign code of conscience.

In Lois Ames's biographical note that concludes the Bantam edition of *The Bell Jar*, there are striking details about Plath's life. We learn about her tenacity; she submitted forty-five pieces to *Seventeen* magazine before her first short story was finally published.

Forty-five.

For anyone who has ever received a rejection slip from a publisher, there is a certain incredulity that attends this fact; what manner of person was this who took rejection again, and again?

Forty-five.

And then there is the familiar presence of intuition as a critical factor in creative breakthrough. Writing to a friend about her work on *The Bell Jar*, Sylvia described how her illumination arrived not when she was trying to solve the novel problem, but when she was thinking about a new edition of poetry:

I have been wanting to do this for ten years but had a terrible block about Writing A Novel. Then suddenly in beginning negotiations with a New York publisher for an American edition of my poems, the dykes broke and I stayed awake all night seized by fearsome excitement, saw how it should be done, started the next day & go every morning to my borrowed study as to an office & belt out more of it.

Preparation. Incubation. Illumination. It reads like an illustration for Wallas's creativity model. So it should come as no surprise that the Verification came next. Plath wrote:

During the past three months the novel has progressed very satisfactorily, according to my drafted schedule. I have worked through several rough drafts to a final version of Chapters 5 through 8, completing a total of 105 pages of the novel in all, and have outlined in detail Chapters 9 through 12.

As we read through *The Bell Jar* today, whether for the fourth time or the whateverth time, we are resurprised by the freshness and immediacy of the writing, by the authenticity of the pain, by the piercing reality of the sentences.

Beyond the existential impact of the novel, though, there is Sylvia Plath's sheer, shimmering talent, and this talent is nowhere more visible than in her similes.

Reading *The Bell Jar* is like reading Dante's *Paradiso*—after a point, one becomes irritated by Dante's apparent callous indifference to the work of future poets; in the *Paradiso* he has greedily used up all possible images of light, exhausted them, ransacked the creative mines for images of light, squandered them by the hundreds, leaving nothing for future poets to invent, leaving nothing but used images and empty image wrappers.

The Bell Jar is like that. It is a tour-de-force of similes, is supported by a frame of similes, is the manifest symphony of a simile genius.

Sylvia Plath was a simile genius.

On the first page of *The Bell Jar*, she wrote that New York's morning freshness evaporated *like the tail end of a sweet dream*. Below, Sylvia-Esther describes seeing a cadaver and being unable to shake the grotesque image from her mind: "and pretty soon I felt as though I were carrying that cadaver's head around with me on a string, like some black noseless balloon stinking of vinegar."

OK, we think, so that's how it's going to be. Similes red of tooth and claw, no holds barred, write to the death.

Then the next sentence: "I knew something was wrong with me that summer, because all I could think about was the Rosenbergs . . ."

Then, in page after page, the wrong-with-me similes descend in a torrent of anguished imagery. The clothes in Esther's closet are hanging *limp as fish*, a girl on scholarship ends up steering New York *like her own private car*, Esther goes back and forth to work *like a numb trolleybus*, all the while feeling very still and very empty, *the way the eye of a tornado must feel, moving dully along in the middle of the surrounding hullabaloo.*

One of my troubles, Sylvia-Esther writes, was Doreen:

I'd never known a girl like Doreen before. Doreen came from a society girl's college down South and had bright white hair standing out in a cotton candy fluff round her head and blue eyes like transparent agate marbles, hard and polished and just about indestructible, and a mouth set in a perpetual sneer.

The description is swift and powerful, like Mark Twain's description of vine-haired Pap at Huck's window, and we are stunned by the eyes like polished, indestructible marbles. Indestructible eyes. It is an amazing adjective in an equally amazing simile.

Doreen, Esther writes, "had intuition. Everything she said was like a secret voice speaking straight out of my own bones."

Standing on the street, Esther and Doreen see girls from the magazine leaving for a party in one cab after another, *like a wedding party with nothing but bridesmaids.* At a bar Esther feels herself melting into the shadows *like the negative of a person I'd never seen before in my life.* A predatory man lurks around Doreen, staring at her *the way people stare at the great white macaw in the zoo, waiting for it to say something human.* Watching this, Esther feels the silence shooting up around me on all sides, *thick as jungle grass.*

Similes after similes, similes within similes.

The mass of droll, grotesque, cynical similes increases until the accumulated unreality of these figures of speech seems more real than the reality that is their referent. Background and foreground reverse polarity, and we are drawn through the rabbit hole of simile into the lost mind of Esther Greenwood aka Sylvia Plath.

Sylv-Esther.

Esther and Doreen go to Lenny's apartment, where the drops on the drinks are *like sweat,* where Esther sits on a bed and tries to look devout and impassive *like some businessman I once saw watching an Algerian belly dancer,* where Esther's drink tastes like dead water. Esther flees the apartment, and the stale heat of the New

York sidewalk hits her in the face *like a last insult.* She arrives back at her hotel, and the elevator doors shut *like a noiseless accordion.* Far below her window, the UN balances itself in the dark, *like a weird green Martian honeycomb.* The china-white bedside telephone sits, *dumb as a death's head.* Doreen returns drunk to the apartment; her white hair falls down from its dark roots *like a hula fringe.*

On and on the similes go, linking their insidious tendrils like dendrites in a brain, until the effect pervades the affect. Reading a lovely story, Esther wants to crawl between those black lines of print *the way you crawl through a fence.* From the page of a magazine, the face of Eisenhower beams up at Esther, bald and blank *as the face of a fetus in a bottle.* The thought that she might kill herself forms in her mind coolly *as a tree or a flower.* In a photography session, Esther suddenly feels limp and betrayed, *like the skin shed by a terrible animal.* At a party, the faces are *empty as plates.* Esther's date is a woman hater; she is dealt to him, *like a playing card in a pack of identical cards.* The music breaks over her *like a rainstorm.* Her date's face is alien and pained, *like a refugee's.* When she strikes him in the face, it is *like hitting the steel plate of a battleship.*

Later, through the train window, Connecticut flashes past, looking *like a colossal junkyard.* Her white eyelet blouse has frills at the shoulder, floppy *as the wings of a new angel.* She reaches for the telephone to say she will come take a course, but her hand stops short, *as if it had collided with a pane of glass.* Her mother's pin curls glitter on her head, *like a row of little bayonets.* A plan begins leaping through her head, *like a family of scatty rabbits.* Unable to sleep, Esther sees her eyelids hang the raw screen of their tiny vessels in front of her *like a wound.* She crawls between the mattress and the padded bedstead and lets the mattress fall across her *like a tombstone.*

Esther's descent into hellish psychology continues, conveyed on a current of hellish, disturbing similes. When Doctor Gordon asks Esther what is wrong, she turns his words over suspiciously, *like round, sea-polished pebbles that might suddenly put out a claw and change into something else.* Doctor Gordon's pencil taps on a green blotter, *like a stalled walking stick.* She eats a peanut, and it tastes dead, *like a bit of old tree bark.* Before her first shock treatment, Esther tries to ask Doctor Gordon what it will be like, but no words come from her mouth; her eyes widen and stare at his smiling, familiar face that floats before her *like a plate full of assurances.* The shock treatment begins, and something bends down and shakes her *like the end of the world.* The great jolts drub her until she thinks her bones will break and the sap fly out of me *like a split plant.* After the shock treatment, she tries to concentrate, but her mind glides off *like a skater, into a large empty space, and pirouettes there, absently.*

In Plath's gallery of comparisons, even the bodies are bodiless; human things are described as though they had no connection to life; all objects are presented in cold code, like pallid display specimens. On the beach, Esther finds a shell, thick, smooth, *big as a thumb joint.* Shanties have sprung up on the beach *like a crop of tasteless mushrooms.* The dry stones clank together *like money.* A wave draws back, *like a hand,* and then touches Esther's foot; the wave seems to come from the sea floor itself:

> ...where blind fish ferried themselves by their own light through the great polar cold. I saw sharks' teeth

and whales' earbones littered about like gravestones.

Esther swims out into the waves with Cal, who turns back. She watches from the sea as he drags himself slowly from the sea onto the shore. Against the khaki-colored sand and the green shore wavelets, his body is dissected for a moment, *like a white worm*. Esther goes to find her father's grave, but the graveyard disappoints her; it is at the outskirts of town, on low ground, *like a rubbish dump*.

Esther attempts suicide, crawling into the crawlspace of her home and gulping down a bottle of sleeping pills. Later, she wakes up when a chisel cracks down on her eye and a slit of light opens, *like a mouth or a wound*. She tries to roll away from the light, but hands wrap around her limbs *like mummy bands*, and she can not move. She is in a hospital, where she breaks a thermometer and watches the balls of toxic mercury that tremble *like celestial dew*.

The comparisons envelop the reader like a seamless membrane of repulsion, reviving in fiction the alienated and self-destructive nonfiction that had been Sylvia Plath's close experience. A chauffeur's neck is *Spam-colored*, physics formulas are *scorpion-like*, a rock bulges from the sea *like a gray skull*, forgetfulness is *like a kind of snow*, a river that she could have jumped to her death in passes by *like an untouched drink*, the white highlights of Bloomingdale jewelry glint *like imitation stars*, a tall nurse has buck teeth and an acne-pitted face that looks *like maps of the craters of the moon*, and Esther's second shock treatment wipes her out *like chalk on a blackboard*.

After the wipe-out, Esther sees Joan, who has eyes *like two gray, goggly pebbles*, who hangs about Esther *like a large and breathless fruitfly*, and whose voice slides down Esther's spine *like a shaft*. Joan fascinates Esther; it is *like observing a Martian, or a particularly warty toad*.

In a better world, with better stories, Sylvia Plath would have emerged from this haunted landscape of doomsday similes to renewed life, to—as poet Howard Nemerov has said—find again the world, where loveliness adorns intelligible things. It did not happen that way.

Plath's own simile described it best; at the philosophical center of *The Bell Jar*, where the fiction axis crosses the nonfiction axis, Sylvia-Esther wrote, "To the person in the bell jar, blank and stopped as a dead baby, the world itself is the bad dream." In Sylvia Plath's life, the bell jar did descend again, closing her off from the circulating air; her world continued to be a bad dream, a blank dream, and the person in her personality became stopped.

In one of her last poems, "The Moon and the Yew Tree," Sylvia Plath wrote, This is the light of the mind, cold and planetary. The trees of the mind, she wrote, are black.

Fumy, spiritous mists, she wrote, inhabit this place.

On February 11, 1963, Sylvia Plath stopped this place.

Her mind had been a cold and planetary place, which black trees and fumy, spiritous mists inhabited. The words of her mind, mined from the similes that litter *The Bell Jar*, were indigenous, like *noseless, stinking, limp, numb, silence, thick, dead, insult, noiseless, weird, dumb, death's head, blank, bald, fetus, terrible, identical, refugee, steel, floppy, junkyard, collided, wound, claw, stalled, split, empty, absently, thumb joint, tasteless, mushroom, clank, earbone, gravestone, tombstone, dissected, rubbish, slit, mummy, untouched, crater,* chalk, *goggly, breathless, spine, warty,* and *stopped.*

These were the words of the mind.

Cold and planetary.

It would be easy to miss the importance of Sylvia Plath's work, easy to file her away as an early feminist who piloted integrity into the latter half of the century.

But as important as her work is in this regard, it is not finally as a political pioneer that she will excite the care of those who really read her; it is as a writer, as a poet of striking power, who happened also to write a novel. When we read Plath's dazzling similes, or her signature lines of poetry, we recognize that we are in the presence of a real poet; we have wandered into the same scape of human genius that we recall from our encounter with Shakespeare. In fact, there are times when only lines from Shakespeare seem clearly similar to Plath's poetry.

In *Macbeth* we recoiled from the hissing and cracking of "Fillet of a fenny snake, in the cauldron boil and bake," and in "The Moon and the Yew Tree" we feel a chill of horror when the hissing, gaseous consonants of *Fumy, spiritous mists inhabit this place* rise all around us. In Plath's cold and planetary mind, the sounds of

fffffffffffffff

sssssssssss

hhhhhhhhhhhhhh

thththththththth

iiiiiiiiiii

rise and envelop us, insidiously, in lethal consonance, and where there seemed to be no poetry, no obvious rhyme, we are suddenly surrounded by a lost symphony of spiritous sounds.

The place is inhabited.

By a poet.

And Shakespeare himself would love these lines, whose technique is hidden from vulgar view, leaving no telltale rhyme or clocky meter to attract detection. Even in meter, though, *Fumy, spiritous mists inhabit this place* is built of trochees, those cruel anti-twins of iambs, that cancel the safe iambic lope of normal English languge. FUmy, SPIRit ous MISTSin HABit THIS PLACE. Take out the *ous* and make the PLACE a place, and you have trochaic pentameter.

Subtle.

Sylvia Plath was a poet.

A simile genius.

A brilliant writer, who might have been saved if she had lived to see ten more years of medical progress.

But down came the bell jar, and the words stopped.

For us, there are the poems and *The Bell Jar* and the ability to love words that for all their stark and wasted sadness are still powerful and especially beautiful.

TWENTY

The Road Ahead

Bill Gates

We are watching something historic happen, and it will affect the world seismically, rocking us the same way the discovery of the scientific method, the invention of printing and the arrival of the Industrial Age did.

-Bill Gates, *The Road Ahead*

That is how Gill Gates, the CEO of Microsoft Corporation, describes the coming of the Information Superhighway in his book *The Road Ahead*, which he wrote with the assistance of Nathan Myhrvold and Peter Rinearson. Gates predicts that the information road ahead will bring revolutionary changes to the lives of people everywhere, in every nation, in every walk of life. It will, Gates says, be something historic, like the invention of printing.

Printing.

Well, we think, careful here; the invention of printing—and Gates's other analogies, the discovery of the scientific method and the arrival of the Industrial Age—was an alpha moment, one of the few most profound and radical changes in human history. European society before and after printing was so dramatically different that it is difficult even to compare the two. Can the information highway change our lives as dramatically as that? I mean, we already have the microcomputer and the

Internet, so how different can this info highway world be?

Very different.

The chances are that you already have an opinion about Bill Gates. Certainly, he has received no end of media coverage as CEO and founder of Microsoft Corporation, the industry giant that has more than six billion dollars a year in sales. Much of what we have seen in the media about Bill Gates has been negative; at least, it has been negatively intended. His new house has been widely covered, with undertones of its being the most fabulous and pretentious house in America, which it is not and was not intended to be. His relationship with Apple Computer has been portrayed as a kind of Star Wars/Trek Evil Empire story, with Apple as the rebel alliance trying to save creativity from the borg-like cybercorporation Microsoft. You almost expect Microsoft headquarters to be some vast black cube, where zombie-nerds stagger in stupors, with their hearts switched to OFF. Recently, when Gates brought Microsoft to the rescue of Apple and the Macintosh at the request of and in cooperation with the beatified Apple saint Steve Jobs, members of the audience booed when Gates's face appeared on a screen at the front of the room.

Concerning these boos, a slight discursion: I am a long-time Macintosh user, typing this article on my seventh Macintosh. In my home now are four Macintoshes, and my daughter has one at college. In my office at work, I have both a PC and a Macintosh. Over the years, I have watched the relationship between Apple and Microsoft evolve, have seen Gates vilified by Macintosh enthusiasts, and have read interviews with Steve Jobs in which he severely criticized the Gates/Microsoft approach to software. Jobs's main complaint seemed to be that Microsoft, as seen in its MS-DOS and Windows operating systems and other PC software, has no taste. No creativity. No style.

Though I admire Jobs and applaud his courage in working with Gates for the salvation of Apple, I always have been a bit puzzled by this attitude. After all, Gates and Microsoft helped make the Macintosh the computer it became by providing much of its earliest and most dazzling software (Microsoft Word, Microsoft Excel) at a time when there was nothing in the PC world to equal it. Businesses bought Macintoshes just to be able to run the Microsoft Excel spreadsheet program. Once the PCs gained power, Gates and company wrote software for them, too. As it turned out, Apple made a number of marketing errors, the PCs gained market share, and Gates became identified as the enemy.

So it does not seem so strange to me that Gates and Jobs would cooperate; Gates was always there; he was part of Apple's early success story. He was present at the creation. He is still there.

Today, Gates is embroiled in a struggle with Washington, which wants him not to include his Internet browser, Internet Explorer, with his operating system, Windows. In this interpretation, Gates is viewed as a monopolist, a neoMorgan who nefariously gobbles up every quivering competitor. Every day, it seems, we read in the paper that the borg empire, Microsoft, has acquired another telecommunications company, spreading its tendrils of control and influence methodically into every one of the wheres that will soon coalesce into the information highway. And all of us pale at the power of the Dark Side.

The real Bill Gates, who will still look twenty-six when he is fifty-two, was born in Seattle in 1955.

He went to college at Harvard, where he vied to get the highest grades while going to the fewest classes. With his friend Paul Allen, he left Harvard and in 1975 founded Microsoft, which was the first company to write operating software for microcomputers. He was in the right place at the right time.

Some of this story is included in *The Road Ahead*, but surprisingly little. *The Road Ahead* is not Bill Gates's autobiography. It is also not the story of Microsoft. It is not about the computer revolution, although some of that, too, is inevitably included. *The Road Ahead*—is this surprising or not?—is actually focused on one thing: the information highway that will transform our lives in less than one generation.

Yeah, right.

Well, listen to Gates:

... The highway is going to happen.

Big changes used to take generations or centuries. This one won't happen overnight, but it will move much faster. The first manifestations of the information highway will be apparent in the United States by the millennium. Within a decade there will be widespread effects....

You'll know the information highway has become part of your life when you begin to resent it if information is not available via the network. One day you'll be hunting for the repair manual for your bicycle and you'll be annoyed that the manual is a paper document that you could misplace. You'll wish it were an interactive electronic document, with animated illustrations and a video tutorial, always available on the network.

By the millennium. That, as they say on Wall Street, is PDQ. I know, they do not actually say that on Wall Street, but they should. Pretty Durned Quick is when the advance scouts of the info highway will arrive.

In fact, Bill Gates wrote *The Road Ahead* in 1995. Today, in 1997, here I sit, back home again in Indiana, working at a computer that operates at 275 MHz, has an internal 56K modem and an internal Zip drive, CD ROM drive, floppy drive, 6 gigabyte hard drive, 96 megabytes of RAM, and a 17 inch monitor that displays millions, yes millions, of colors. The images on the screen look photographic, and they pop out instantly. The computer plays multimedia CD's and audio CD's. If I put my new Bob Dylan CD into the drive, the sound comes out in stereo, with a speaker under the computer acting as a subwoofer.

With a click of a button, which is not a real button but an icon of a button on the screen, I can summon forth an interactive multimedia encyclopedia, awesome video games, vast dictionaries and brontothesaurases, and word processors that would have amazed anyone just five years ago. In am preparing this text in Aldus PageMaker, and it looks on the screen just like it looks on the printed page.

With another click on another button, a telephone pad appears on the screen, and I can dial my mom's number and hear her voice answer on the computer speaker. When I speak back, the computer's microphone picks up my voice and transmits it to Mom.

With another click, I send handouts for a language arts presentation I will soon do for a school system in a distant state directly to the system office; they are received by the school system's fax machine.

With another click of another button, an Internet

browser opens up, where my customized Internet page immediately presents me with all the things I have previously asked for: weather in my town, in my Mom's town, and where my daughter is in college. I also get scores for just the sports teams (the Dolphins) and leagues (NFL, NBA) I am interested in, news about topics I have selected to be automatically filtered out for me (Bob Dylan, NAGC), business and investment reports about companies I am interested in (Apple, Microsoft, World of Science), television and movie theater listings for my city. Click, and a review of a movie pops up. Click, and a description of a program on the Discovery Channel pops up. Click, and there is a Reuters report about Bob Dylan and the Pope. Click, and the Dolphins's coach, Jimmy Johnson, is quoted as saying he'll keep Dan Marino. Click, and a thirty-day, or ten-day, or year-to-date stock chart pops out on Apple Computer Company; I can add trend lines, moving averages, and print the chart.

With another click of a button, I can ask the web browser (Netscape Navigator is what I usually use, although I am getting curious about the browser from Microsoft, Internet Explorer) to search for anything I am interested in. Click, search for trilobites. Whap, and there are hundreds of websites about trilobites, everything from research and doctoral theses to ads in rock and fossil shops. Click, search for Guy Fawkes, and whap: dozens of articles about Guy Fawkes, with photographs.

With another click, I bring up my email page, and out come e-letters to me from friends and colleagues. Here is one from South Carolina; here is one from Portland. Some of them were sent just moments ago. Quickly, I answer some of them, and click, my answers are on their way.

With another click, I bring up my bank account.

There is my checking, my savings. I see my balances, my recent transactions, my service charges. Click, and I can transfer money from savings to checking. Click, and I pay a bill. Click, and I send money to my daughter's college. I have written fewer than twenty paper checks in six months. Soon, I will write none.

Click.

Click.

Click.

All of this.

It is amazing.

I cannot remember how I lived without these things.

All of this.

And here's the thing: this is NOT the information highway revolution.

This is only the PC era.

This is what will be replaced.

The chances are, you already have an opinion about Bill Gates. The chances are that you view him as he has been portrayed in the media, as a computer megageek whose vision stops at the end of a silicon chip. It is a different thing to read *The Road Ahead* and to see how he portrays himself.

One of the things that stands out in *The Road Ahead* is that Gates is a reader. For everyone who thought that he was just a monitor viewer, this may come as a surprise. Gates's book is filled with references to books, films, historical events, inventions, artists; it is not the work of a technoman who is interested only in software and commercial domination. He began as an encyclopedia reader:

When I was young I loved my family's 1960 *World Book Encyclopedia*. Its heavy bound volumes contained just text and pictures....When I was eight, I began to read the first volume. I was determined to read straight through every volume. I could have absorbed more if it had been easy to read all the articles about the sixteenth century in sequence or all the articles pertaining to medicine. Instead I read about "Garter Snakes," then "Gary, Indiana," then "Gas." But I had a great time reading the encyclopedia anyway and kept at it for five years until I reached the *p*s.

In discussing how the information highway will be able to alert us to new developments in fields that we are interested in, so long as we are willing to provide a profile of our interests, Gates writes:

Why would you want to create such a profile? I certainly don't want to reveal everything about myself, but it would be helpful if an agent knew I wanted to see any safety features the new model Lexus might have added. Or, it could alert me to the publication of a new book by Philip Roth, John Irving, Ernest J. Gaines, Donald Knuth, David Halberstam, or any of my other longtime favorite writers. I would also like to have it signal me when a new book appears on some topic that intersts me: economics and technology, learning theories, Franklin Delano Roosevelt, and biotechnology, to name a few. I was quite stimulated by a book called *The Language Instinct*, written by Steven Pinker, a professor at MIT, and I'd like to know about new books or articles on its ideas.

In talking about teachers who made a difference, Gates

says:

We've all had teachers who made a difference. I had a great chemistry teacher in high school who made his subject immensely interesting. Chemistry seemed enthralling compared to biology. In biology, we were dissecting frogs—just hacking them to pieces, actually—and our teacher didn't explain why. My chemistry teacher sensationalized his subject a bit and promised that it would help us understand the world. When I was in my twenties, I read James D. Watson's *Molecular Biology of the Gene* and decided my high school experience had misled me. The understanding of life is a great subject. Biological information is the most important information we can discover, because over the next several decades it will revolutionize medicine. Human DNA is like a computer program but far, far more advanced than any software ever created. It seems amazing to me now that one great teacher made chemistry endlessly fascinating while I found biology totally boring.

Reading this book initiates a kind of cognitive dissonance. Expecting a tract by MicroMan, we find instead a very readable, approachable book, filled with references not only to the technology of the future but to the friends of our youth: Pompeian fresoes, Cubist paintings, Picasso, James Burke, Gutenberg, Raphael, Modigliani, Levi Strauss & Co., Alexander Graham Bell, Saint-Exupery, La Dolce Vita, Madonna, F. Scott Fitzgerald, Blaise Pascal, Elvis, Forrest Gump, Cecil B. DeMille, Jurassic Park, Stephen Hawking, Ghiberti's Baptistery doors in Florence, *The Lion King*, *The Mask*, Thomas Edison, H.G. Wells, Seurat, James D. Watson,

Richard Feynman, and other familiar names. We expected Gates to be smart; we did not, perhaps, expect him to be so broadly read or so interested both in general intellectual issues and mass culture phenomena. We did not, perhaps, expect him to have a literary sensitivity. Discussing interactive media, Gates says:

> I don't want to choose an ending for *The Great Gatsby* or *La Dolce Vita*. F. Scott Fitzgerald and Fererico Fellini have done that for me. The suspension of disbelief essential to the enjoyment of great fiction is fragile and may not hold up under the heavy-handed use of interactivity. You can't simultaneously control the plot and surrender your imagination to it.

We did not, perhaps, expect him to tell so many interesting things we did not know, such as that "the *Declaration of Independence* was written on a lap desk in Philadelphia," or that the fiber-optic cable that will carry the info highway is so unimaginably clear:

> Fiber is cable made of glass or plastic so smooth and pure that if you looked through a wall of it 70 miles thick, you'd be able to see a candle burning on the other side.

Clearer, in other words, than air.

Do not be misled; *The Road Ahead* is not a groovy new history of Western civilization. It is a book that focuses on the information highway that will revolutionize our lives.

You can tell that from the chapters: A Revolution Begins, The Beginning of the Information Age, Lessons from the Computer Industry, Applications and Appliances, Paths to the Highway, The Content Revolution, Implications for Business, Friction-Free Capitalism, Education: The Best Investment, Plugged In at Home, Race for the Gold, and Critical Issues.

In the first chapter, "A Revolution Begins," Gates recalls the early days (the late 1960s) when computers did not even have monitors. "I wrote my first software program when I was thirteen years old," he says. It was for playing tic-tac-toe. Gates reviews the precocious path that led him into the computer age, but he draws a distinction between the present computer era and what is to come. "Personal computers have already altered work habits," he says, "but they haven't really changed our lives much yet." The information highway will:

> Before Gutenberg, there were only about 30,000 books on the entire continent of Europe, nearly all Bibles or biblical commentary. By 1500, there were more than 9 million, on all sorts of topics. Handbills and other printed matter affected politics, religion, science, and literature. For the first time, those outside the canonical elite had access to written information.
>
> The information highway will transform our culture as dramatically as Gutenberg's press did the Middle Ages.

How? Throughout *The Road Ahead* and in the companion CD-ROM, Gates gives guesses, clues, and examples. Stressing that much of the coming change can not yet be imagined, Gates tells us that companies that fail to make their work global will not be able to lead, that we will be able to browse through thousands of libraries, that our idea of what a document is will be redefined when most original documents can no longer be printed on paper because they originate as multimedia documents, that "people, machines, entertainment, and information services will all be accessible," and that "You will be able to stay in touch with anyone, anywhere, who wants to stay in touch with you."

Gates observes that the information highway will require billions of dollars in investment to connect all homes and businesses together with the fiber-optic cable that is required, but he points out that:

> The outlay will be no greater than that for other infrastructures we take for granted. The roads, water mains, sewers, and electrical connections that run to a house each cost as much.

For anyone who mistakenly thinks that today's Internet is the arrival of the highway, Gates has a striking comparison:

> Today's Internet is not the information highway I imagine, although you can think of it as the beginning of the highway. An analogy is the Oregon Trail.... You could easily say the Oregon Trail was the start of today's highway system.

For all of us who are astounded by what our computers can do now that they are attached to the Internet, this is a shock. Will the information highway be as much greater than today's Internet as the modern highway system is greater than the rutted wagon trail to Oregon? More so.

Videoconferencing will be as standard as using a copier.

Bills will not be printed on paper and mailed. They will arrive in your email box, where you will pay them or challenge them with a click.

You will have to look twice to tell whether you are looking at a window or an electronic monitor.

You will not be sure whether the person you are videotalking to is a *homo sapiens* or an electronic social interface. Perhaps the interace will tell you it is human, as a joke.

For millions of jobs, you will be able to live anywhere and still work anywhere because electronically, you will always be everywhere. Driving to work will be replaced by clicking to work.

In millions of instances, it will not matter where a business is located: "stores and services that until now have profited just because they are 'there"—in a particular geographic location—may find they have lost that advantage."

There will be video on demand. You will be able to watch anything at any time. And the video will be interactive:

If you are watching the movie *Top Gun* and think Tom Cruise's aviator sunglasses look really cool, you'll be able to pause the movie and learn about the glasses or even buy them on the spot.

Gates's thinking streams on and on. It is interesting to see that even for Gates, it is difficult to imagine the vast changes, surely to come, that are not obvious. Gates repeatedly cautions us to expect the unexpected. I found myself thinking, if we now have cellular phones that blanket the world for audio communications, will we also one day have a cellular video system that blankets the world for vision? Will I be able to watch my Mom as she goes from site to site on her trip to Italy? Will

I be able to conduct video explorations of any city I want, turning left and right and moving forward at will, with live video providing the feed and each next camera picking up the signal from the previous one, like cell phone systems do? Turn left, go forward to the doors of the Louvre. If you enter, there will be a charge of $2.00 on your bank account. Do you accept? Yes. Click, click.

The Road Ahead is filled with interesting facts, ideas, and predictions. He describes his early interest in computers. Gates says the new technology "will eliminate distance." He provides an wonderful explanation of how binary code works. He explains "Moore's Law":

> In 1965, Gordon Moore, who later cofounded Intel with Bob Noyce, predicted that the capacity of a computer chip would double every year....Ten years later, his forecast proved true, and he then predicted the capacity would double every two years. To this day his predictions have held up, and the average—a doubling every eighteen months—is referred to among engineers as Moore's Law.
>
> No experience in our everyday life prepares us for the implications of a number that doubles a great number of times—exponential improvements.

To illustrate, Gates tells the fable of King Shirham of India, who wanted to reward a valued minister. The minister asked for one grain of wheat for the first square of a chessboard, two grains for the next square, and twice each next value until the chessboard was filled with grains. A chessboard is eight squares by eight, and as Gates observes:

It is safe to say that the king broke his promise to the minister. The final square would have gotten 18,446,744,073,709,551,615 grains of wheat on the board, and required 584 billion years of counting. Current estimates of the age of the earth are around 4.5 billion years.

Gates points out that Moore's law is likely to hold for another twenty years, making computations that now take more than a day faster than ten seconds.

Sometimes Gates reveals elements of his business mind, as when he describes why Microsoft licensed its software at extremely low prices:

> It was our belief that money could be made betting on volume. We adapted our programming languages, such as our version of BASIC, to each machine. We were very responsive to all the hardware manufacturers' requests. We didn't want to give anyone a reason to look elsewhere. We wanted choosing Microsoft software to be a no-brainer.

Sometimes, he describes, with a tacit incredulity, the stupidity of those who can not adapt to change or to ideas that will improve things for everyone. In working with IBM, Microsoft solicited ideas for changes in its new software:

> I remember change request #221: "Remove fonts from product. Reason: Enhancement to product's substance." Someone at IBM didn't want the PC operating system to offer multiple typefaces because a particular IBM mainframe printer couldn't handle them.

Sometimes Gates explains positions that seem paradoxical, such as his recruiting managers whose companies have failed:

> In recent years, Microsoft has deliberately hired a few managers with experience in failing companies. When you're failing you're forced to be creative, to dig deep and think, night and day. I want some people around who have been through that. Microsoft is bound to have failures in the future, and I want people here who have proved they can do well in tough situations.

Sometimes, he provides insights into the things that limit our thinking, as in this story of a team trying to write handwriting recognition software:

> Another time, when the team thought they had created a program that worked, they came proudly to demonstrate their achievement to me. It didn't work at the demonstration. Everyone on the project happened to be right-handed, and the computer, which was programmed to look at the strokes in the writing, couldn't interpret the very different ones in my left-handed penmanship.

Sometimes, he gives tantalizing hints about the immense changes that are approaching, as in his discussion about how the concept of a document will be redefined:

> By the end of the decade a significant percentage of documents, even in offices, won't even be fully printable on paper. They will be like a movie or a song is today. You will still be able to print a two-

dimensional view of its content, but it will be like reading a musical score instead of experiencing an audio recording.

Here is Gates's description of what will happen to the movie rental industry:

Videos, which tend to be watched only once, will continue to be rented, but probably not from stores. Instead, consumers will shop on the information highway to find movies and other programs deliverable on demand.

Interestingly, Gates devotes an entire chapter of *The Road Ahead* to education. Entitled "Education: The Best Investment," this chapter gives us a glimpse at the nature of change in education that the information highway will bring. Gates says that "information technology will bring mass customization to learning. Multimedia documents and easy-to-use authoring tools will enable teachers to mass-customize a curriculum." Gates says that "Every member of society, including every child, will have more information easily at hand than anyone has today.... Education will become a very individual matter."

Gates "emphatically and unequivocally" denies that the information highway will replace teachers; rather, he says, "The highway will bring together the best work of countless teachers and authors for everyone to share."

In his discussion of testing and the effects of tests on students, Gates notes that students who experience failures on tests often are injured in the process:

Tests can cause a student to develop a negative attitude toward all education. The interactive network will allow students to quiz themselves anytime, in a risk-free environment. A self-administered quiz is a form of self-exploration....Testing will become a positive part of the learning process. A mistake won't call forth a reprimand; it will trigger the system to help the student overcome his misunderstanding.

Gates gets us to imagine the future quality of educational software, noting that "as textbook budgets and parental spending shift to interactive material, there will be thousands of new software companies working with teachers to create entertainment-quality interactive learning materials."

"The highway," Gates says, "will allow new methods of teaching and much more *choice*."

The italics are not mine.

They are Gates's.

But if he had not put *choice* in italics, I would have.

Choice, we have seen repeatedly, is a powerful function of intelligence, and it varies positively; the more intelligent a person is, the more choice he or she needs in order to be happy and productive. Great teachers need authority to be creative, rather than to merely implement an approved curriculum. Great students need choice in their learning, in order to follow the dynamic of their internal learning passions. Choice and brilliance go hand in hand. Every profound study of gifted education recognizes choice as one of the imperatives, a sine qua non.

Much more choice, Gates says. Some pages later, he ends his chapter on education in the information age with these words:

I enjoyed school but I pursued my strongest interests outside the classroom. I can only imagine how access to this much information would have changed my own school experience. The highway will alter the focus of education from the institution to the individual.

The highway will alter the focus of education from the institution to the individual.

Choice.

What is coming will be different from what we know today.

Today, the choices are not ours.

Consider the model of television programming. Soon, the present system will seem unimaginably paleolithic. What, you could only see a movie at specified times? You had to get a schedule from the newspaper to find out when programs were showing? Weird.

How would you feel if the phone system worked like the television system, and you could only call certain people at certain times, which had to be looked up in the newspaper? How would you feel if you couldn't call who you wanted, when you wanted?

Soon, you will feel that way about the television system.

And about every other system, education included.

The focus will be altered from the institution to the individual.

You will choose.

You will choose when.

You will choose what.

You will choose how.

You.

Choice.

Individual.

The information highway will bring shocking new developments to society, enabling millions of people, for better or even for worse (Gates thinks better), to see, find, and express things that no one alive can control now..

Institutional schedules will begin vanishing, to be replaced by individual choices, customization, freedom, and interactivity. New hybrid machines that combine cellular phones, networks, and computers will give us virtual highway-gates that we carry with us, enabling us to do business, communicate with friends and associates, play games, and learn, no matter what time it is or where we are.

As Gutenberg's book brought Western civilization into a new intellectual world, the information highway will bring profound intellectual changes to our ways of life, our daily processes, our ways of interacting with friends, our self-image, our economy, and our methods of education.

The Road Ahead is the surprising work of a gifted individual whose life and abilities identify him as a kind of Tireseus of our civilization. His book says extraordinary things in a soft, mild-mannered voice and is essential reading for every educator.

And the book, of course, is only a pale, silent, still, two-dimensional version of the accompanying CD; you'll have to explore it to see the original document.

TWENTY-ONE

*Narrative of the Life of Frederick Douglass,
An American Slave, Written by Himself*

Frederick Douglass

W.E.B. Du Bois, the first African American to earn a Ph.D from Harvard University, wrote about Frederick Douglass in his 1903 classic analysis of the race problem in American society, *The Souls of Black Folk*. Criticizing Booker T. Washington for failing to assert the rights of African Americans, Du Bois wrote:

Here, led by Remond, Nell, Wells-Brown, and Douglass, a new period of self-assertion and self-development dawned. To be sure, ultimate freedom and assimilation was the ideal before the leaders, but the assertion of the manhood rights of the Negro by himself was the main reliance, and John Brown's raid was the extreme of its logic. After the war and emancipation, the great form of Frederick Douglass, the greatest of American Negro leaders, still led the host. Self-assertion, especially in political lines, was the main programme, and behind Douglass came Elliot, Bruce, and Langston, and the Reconstruction politicians, and, less conspicuous but of greater social significance, Alexander Crummell and Bishop Daniel Payne.

Then came the Revolution of 1876, the suppression of the Negro votes, the changing and shifting of ideals, and the seeking of new lights in the great night. Douglass, in his old age, still bravely stood for the ideals of his early manhood,—ultimate assimilation through self-assertion, and on no other terms.

The great form of Frederick Douglass, Du Bois wrote, still led the host. The greatest of American Negro leaders, Du Bois wrote. In his old age, Du Bois wrote, Douglass still stood for the ideals of his early manhood.

History, or is it just time? has a way of settling the dust. Clearing the view. Bringing the salient facts to the fore. As we look back today from the distance of nearly two centuries to the scene of Douglass's childhood—he was born in 1817 or 1818—we find it difficult to believe the life that emerged. To say that Douglass overcame ignorance does not begin to describe the problem. As he explained in his now-classic autobiography, *Narrative of the Life of an American Slave, Written by Himself*, Douglass did not even know his own birthday:

> I have no accurate knowledge of my age, never having seen any authentic record containing it. By far the larger part of the slaves know as little of their ages as horses know of theirs, and it is the wish of most masters within my knowledge to keep their slaves thus ignorant. I do not remember to have ever met a slave who could tell of his birthday.

Douglass wrote that it always made him feel bad, not to know his own birthday. We wince, but it is nothing; Douglass not only did not know his own birthday, he never knew who his father was—except that everyone said it was a white man and probably his master—and he never really knew his mother:

I never saw my mother, to know her as such, more than four or five times in my life; and each of these times was overly short in duration, and at night....She made her journeys to see me in the night, travelling the whole distance on foot, after the performance of her day's work....I do not recollect of ever seeing my mother by the light of day. She was with me in the night. She would lie down with me, and get me to sleep, but long before I waked she was gone....Death soon ended what little we could have while she lived, and with it her hardships and suffering.

It is impossible for us to imagine accurately the brutalizing experiences that Douglass suffered in his childhood. What would be our reaction today, if we were to actually see someone whipped? Douglass was whipped, and he had to witness others being whipped:

Mr. Severe was rightly named: he was a cruel man. I have seen him whip a woman, causing the blood to run half an hour at the time; and this too, in the midst of her crying children, pleading for their mother's release. He seemed to take pleasure in manifesting his fiendish barbarity.

Douglass was hungry, and he was cold:

I suffered much from hunger, but much more from cold. In hottest summer and coldest winter, I was kept almost naked—no shoes, no stockings, no jacket, no trousers, nothing on but a coarse tow linen shirt, reaching only to my knees. I had no bed. I must have perished with cold, but that, the coldest nights, I used to steal a bag which was used for carrying corn to the mill. I would crawl into this bag, and there sleep on the cold, damp, clay floor, with my head in and feet out. My feet have been so cracked with the frost, that the pen with which I am writing might be laid in the gashes.

A motherless slave boy, shivering with cold, sleeping in a corn sack on a dirt floor; this was Douglass's state in the 1820s. Within a decade, he taught himself to read and write. In 1838 he escaped to the North, became a world-famous author and speaker, and advised President Lincoln and President Johnson. In 1871 President Grant appointed him Assistant Secretary of the Santo Domingo Commission.

If ever a child's life demonstrated the transition from gifted potential to developed talent, as we have recently seen it described in Gagne's model, it was Frederick Douglass. How could this small boy possibly have overcome all of the obstacles in his path, the ignorance and poverty, the brutality of slavery, the hostile environment, the laws that made it illegal for him to be educated, the cold, the hunger, the lack of clothing, the lack of parents—everything. How did this miserable boy, Frederick Augustus Washington Baily, become Frederick Douglass, the great form in American history?

There are at least two factors that stand out. One is the enormous intelligence that is especially evident in Douglass's gift with language. In every paragraph of his *Narrative*, his brilliance as a narrator is manifest. And somehow, even when he is describing the most pitiful or tragic events, his voice carries an authority and a status that pervades the language, raining contempt on the slave system and the slave holders, exposing the brutality and degradation of the slave holders' personalities, and showing the humanity of the slaves, despite their horrid conditions. To say that Douglass is self-assertive is to understate.

In addition to Douglass's gift with language, there is his defiance. From his early childhood, Douglass possessed a will to live, a kind of insistent authenticity that would not let him settle for slavery, not let him settle for definitions that minimized the importance of his life, and not let him settle for cruelty and abuse visited upon him, no matter what so-called authority attempted to control him. Douglass described the turning point of his life—the day that he stood up to Covey, the slave-breaker: "You have seen how a man was made a slave; you shall see how a slave was made a man." Douglass had been at odds with Covey for days, and had implored his master to take him back from the slave-breaker, but his request was refused. He was working in a barn, when:

Mr. Covey entered the stable with a long rope; and just as I was half out of the loft, he caught hold of my legs, and was about tying me. As soon as I found what he was up to, I gave a sudden spring, and as I did so, he holding to my legs, I was brought sprawling on the stable floor. Mr. Covey seemed now to think he had me, and could do what he pleased; but at this moment—from whence came the spirit I don't know—I resolved to fight; and, suiting my action to the resolution, I seized Covey hard by the throat; and as I did so, I rose. He held on to me, and I to him. My resistance was so entirely unexpected, that Covey seemed taken all aback. He trembled like a leaf.

Covey called out for help, but to no avail:

We were at it for nearly two hours. Covey at length let me go, puffing and blowing at a great rate, saying that if I had not resisted, he would not have whipped me half so much. The truth was, that he had not whipped me at all....The whole six months afterwards, that I spent with Mr. Covey, he never laid the weight of his finger upon me in anger.

In Frederick Douglass's life, we see much for our gifted children to note. His final victory over disadvantage is an inspiring display of the power of ability and determination, and his classic *Narrative* is an essential text in the story of gifted education.

If Douglass could propel himself to extraordinary achievement, not only without advantages but with the disadvantages stacked against him, what might we accomplish with our children if we can find the way to create advantages for them, or even to become advantages for them.

Curiously, for someone of the extreme mental and moral stature of Frederick Douglass, disadvantage might be a motivating factor. Douglass was rightly infuriated at his life's circumstance; he knew that it was an offense to his dignity and to his true identity as a powerful and intelligent human being, and he responded with overwhelming force, to the benefit of the entire country.